DIARY OF A DANGEROUS VISION

Once again, to my best friends Michele, Sam and Beth.

You know what? I love you all very much!

Diary of a Dangerous Vision

Mad for Jesus
(the vision of the Message Trust)
Fully expanded and updated

ANDY HAWTHORNE

survivor

First published by Hodder & Stoughton in 2000
as *Mad for Jesus*
This revised and expanded edition 2004

ISBN 1 84291 184 8

Front cover photo by Howard Barlow

2 3 4 5 6 Printing/Year 08 07 06 05

Published by
KINGSWAY COMMUNICATIONS LTD
Lottbridge Drove, Eastbourne BN23 6NT, England.
Email: books@kingsway.co.uk

Printed in the USA.

Acknowledgements

H uge thanks to Craig Borlase, first of all for being a top bloke and secondly for spending hours sorting out my rather dodgy manuscript. To Richard Johnson and all the noble trustees of the Message, plus respect to all the wonderful Message full-time staff, the office and ops teams, all the Eden workers and not forgetting, of course, Mark Pennells and Zarc Porter. There would not be a Message Trust, Tribe or any of the other ministries we're involved in without you guys and I know it.

Also to all the faithful supporters of the Message over the last few years who have stood with us in our dream to see Manchester thoroughly blitzed with the good news.

Contents

Foreword

$\mathbf{A}$ ndy Hawthorne is one of the most extraordinary people I have met. His passion for Jesus and for telling about Jesus is infectious. The Message, which Andy leads, is a role model for many of us. Their first priority is reaching young people in Manchester. Their second priority is reaching young people in Manchester. Their third priority...!

Andy and the Tribe could have spent the last few years touring the world entertaining Christians and improving their bank balances. Instead they have stayed true to their calling and maintained their passion and as a result seen miracles happen in Manchester that are having an influence around the world. I write this from an Internet cafe in Melbourne Australia, where last night I met up with the team that are planting an Eden project here in the inner city. This is a wonderful initiative pioneered by Andy in Manchester to repopulate the inner cities with passionate, dedicated young Christian youth workers.

I have counted Andy a good friend and brother for some years now. Working with him may be a few things, but it is not boring! I swear my life expectancy has decreased significantly and I blame him for all the grey that is appearing. Andy is always inspiring and always challenging. So is *Diary of a Dangerous Vision.* In this book you will not only find the exciting story of the Message but also crucial reflections and biblical teaching that equip you to run your race. One of Andy's passions is to see a generation of Bible-honouring, Jesus-loving, Spirit-filled Christians proclaiming Him in word and action to a broken and hurting world. That is the motivation for this book. It is authentic. I warmly commend it to you.

Mike Pilavachi

Introduction:
Barefoot in India

Turn the clocks back a hundred years and Christianity looked a little different: around two-thirds of the world's Christians lived in Europe. God wasn't too happy with this situation, so He got to work on the hearts of His people, giving them a great desire to spread the good news about Jesus to the far ends of the globe. In their thousands young men and women literally gave their all to make Jesus known. Instead of Manchester or Madrid, they chose to take the message out to Africa, South America, China, India and beyond. One such missionary pioneer was Captain Robert Hawthorne. In 1883 he bought a one-way ticket to India, not because he was on the run or looking for a fight (at least not with guns). He was with the Salvation Army and he was my great-grandfather.

He had plenty to think about during the three-month voyage; as one of the first Salvation Army missionaries to visit the country, the task that faced him and his two colleagues was immense. Still, he was pretty fired up about it, partly as before he had left, William Booth, the founder of the Salvation Army, urged him to 'get inside their skins'.

Robert had something else to think about. During their leaving ceremony in London, a beautiful young Salvation Army officer stood up and sang a solo. Robert had never seen her before, but in a burst of either cocky arrogance or prophetic holiness, he turned to his two travelling companions and told them that she was the girl he was going to marry. When she became a missionary in India a few years later, they met again, fell in love and got married. Over one hundred years later there are a few more of us Hawthornes around.

When Robert and his co-workers got to India, it wasn't long before they realised that their Salvation Army uniforms were a little out of place. Back in London they were something to be proud of, but in India they reminded the natives of the uniforms worn by the British soldiers who had colonised their country. The Englishmen decided to ditch their precious threads and instead started wearing traditional Indian costume. Gradually they absorbed more influences from the culture that surrounded them: the housing, the food and the customs, even to the point of not wearing any shoes.

Giving up your shoes might not sound like one of the most radical acts around, but when I read a book about Robert and his mates, I realised that it had a big effect on their lives. One of his colleagues wrote this: 'Even when tramping along on a burning road with sharp stones and thorns like darning needles sticking into you, I look up and not down, and the pain and the dreariness go away and I am happy, supremely happy.' That supreme happiness came from the two things that make life worth living: an intimate and personal relationship with Jesus and a burning desire to share this Jesus with others.

Apparently, the young Salvation Army pioneers competed with each other with new ideas and plans to win people over for Christ. Bit by bit they took on more and more of the culture in order to 'become all things to all men to win a few', and it wasn't long before Captain Hawthorne became known as 'Jaibhai' – taking on an Indian name in order to bring people to Christ.

These radical men and women have turned the world upside down. As a result of their commitment and sacrifice, the gospel has exploded all over the world. Instead of most Christians now living in Europe, these days the vast majority live in the far-off places where the pioneers travelled and gave their lives.

I believe that there is a new breed of missionary pioneer being born in Britain right now. Rather than spending three months on a boat to reach the ends of the earth, they are going a few miles down the road. Like the Salvation Army pioneers, though, they are taking a one-way ticket into the toughest places: the inner cities. William Booth encouraged his workers to 'walk back across the bridges', to go against the tide and find the people who needed Jesus the most. There is so much life in the churches of Britain today, so many things to get excited about, but sadly that life is only reaching a tiny fraction of the population. It can't be right that over 65 per cent of the population in this country are considered working class, and yet less than 1 per cent of the church are working class, and it can't be right that in Manchester, our city, my city, 80 per cent of the Christians live in the suburbs alongside 20 per cent of the people, while only 20 per cent of the Christians live in the urban areas next to 80 per cent of the people. What is even more upsetting is that many of those few Christians who do live in the urban areas actually commute out to the suburban churches for their Sunday and mid-week services. Is it any wonder that, as someone put it, 'the meat's going off in the inner city – there's not enough salt. Or it's very dark because there's not enough light'? You might have guessed that this book isn't just the story of the developing work of the Message Trust (but we will have some of that later, and hopefully there will be some lessons to learn from it). It's certainly not the autobiography of me, a 43-year-old evangelist who feels as if he's just getting started. What it is, though, is much simpler: it's a story of a growing group of people who are running with a vision to see Manchester radically changed.

Let's face it, Manchester – the city and the surrounding Greater Manchester area – is long overdue for a bit of change. Many evangelistic organisations describe it as 'one of the hardest places to do a mission in the world', and for years the situation has gone unchecked. As in any major population centre, there are many social and economic problems that face residents. Crime, unemployment and the breakdown of the family are all instantly recognisable, and housing policies of transferring inner-city communities to out of town estates have only made things worse. The church has also faced its own problems, as factions and back-stabbing have sprung up and unity is shunned.

While the social problems are taking longer to sort out, the church has lately been going through something of a turnaround. In 1993 Frank Green, a local minister, was praying with his wife, Debra, about the situation. In 1992 they had been involved in running the city's first March for Jesus. It had been a big success, especially by Manchester's standards, but when they tried to carry it on the following year any previous enthusiasm seemed to have fizzled out. In answer to their frustrated prayers, Frank had an impression of a walled city whose defences had been all but destroyed by continual attack. There were a few strong towers left surrounding the city, and as he watched, he saw new walls spring up between them. As the defences were once again able to resist the enemy, new towers were able to be built inside the city. This immediately made Frank and Debra think of Manchester: if the strong towers were the churches, then walls had to be unity. The inner city was a spiritual wasteland, but it gave them hope that if the churches could unite, then the whole landscape could change. That October they set up Prayer Network and invited all denominations to take part. Ten years later it attracts thousands to its prayer gatherings and is widely considered to be one of the most exciting prayer movements in the country.

Fifteen years ago we started trying to put on city-wide missions, getting the churches of Manchester on board for something called the Message '88. It was at this time that God really spoke to us from the book of Isaiah, chapter 43. These were the verses that really stood out:

> See, I am doing a new thing! Now it springs up; do you not perceive it? I am making a way in the desert and streams in the wasteland. The wild animals honour me, the jackals and the owls, because I provide water in the desert and streams in the wasteland, to give drink to my people, my chosen, the people I formed for myself that they may proclaim my praise.

From those early days onwards God has been telling us that we should aim for the toughest places. The result is that we have concentrated on Manchester, a city that's never seen revival, and one that to so many evangelistic organisations is a spiritual wasteland. We have known that we should concentrate on young people, as they are the biggest problem the church in Britain has got: we just can't hold on to them. If we could only get them to stay in the church once they've started coming, then the church would start to grow again, and we would be taking this nation for Jesus. We know that our target is not just Manchester's nice young people, but those tough ones from the inner city. The wasteland and the desert have been our fields, and this book shows how the vision for them has grown, how it has changed us, and how we want to see this city turned around.

This isn't just a nice idea to keep us from getting bored. We are a bunch of people with a vision – that Manchester is going to be changed. God has confirmed it time and time again, partly through the many other good things that are springing up all over this city. These different components are all part of God's eye, looking down on Manchester right now.

1

Catching the Bug

Fortunately God's work isn't limited to barefoot mad-for-Jesus missionaries in India. He is working all over the world, and at some point in 1960 he was at work in Hambleton Road, Cheadle, saving a housewife called Christine Hawthorne, my mum.

I was only four months old so my memory's a bit of a blank, but my mum tells me that she was so excited about her new faith that she did everything possible to tell my dad about Jesus. He was a streetwise journalist who thought he knew the score about most things and didn't really have much time for Jesus. My mum used to leave tracts lying about the house, and would turn virtually every conversation they had around to Jesus. Even the boiling time of a pan of carrots managed to become an illustration of how God wanted to soften his heart. But all it did was drive a wedge between her and Dad.

My mum's conversion was part of a mini-revival that

was going on in the street. There had been five or six families who had become Christians over a very short period of time, and Bible studies were springing up all the way down the road. Most of this had been sparked off by the work and prayers of a wonderful old lady called Olive Clarke. She's a total saint, and through her there were plenty of housewives who had met with Jesus and were now praying for their husbands.

After about three months of carrot analogies and tracts in the bathroom, a confirmation class started up at the local church. To Mum's astonishment, Dad expressed an interest in going. Halfway through one of the last classes – having argued his way through all the others – he sat down and talked to the curate, Tony Turner. Tony gave him some cheesy analogy about how you never know that a chair is going to hold you up unless you sit on it. He told him that unless he put his faith in God, he would never know if God was able to save him. My dad, worldly wise hack that he was, was gob-smacked by this little analogy. When they went home he told Mum that he wanted to become a Christian. They knelt down by the bed and Dad gave his life to the Lord. Mum says she remembers praying passionately at that time that their three children – myself, Simon and Michael – would all come to know Jesus as well. Despite it looking a bit dodgy at times, God has answered her prayer in full.

Michael was always a bit of a good lad, doing well at school and going on to become Head of English at a big school in Shropshire before selling just about everything

he had and following in his great-grandfather's foot-
steps to serve the Lord full time in India. Simon and I,
however, took a different route. We went to church until
we had a choice not to, preferring teenage rebellion
over boring church. Simon became a bit of a punk,
having purple hair and being the first lad I knew in the
70s to have an earring. He got into things in a big way:
from drugs to trouble with the police. I wasn't too
much of an angel either, and I remember my headmas-
ter telling me at the end of Year 11 that if I ever turned
up at school again I would be trespassing. I don't think
anyone was very surprised when I didn't stay on.
Instead I went and got a job as a cabinet-maker, simply
because the only qualification I got from school was an
O-level in woodwork. I had wasted my education,
despite the fact that when I was 12 I had made a
commitment to Jesus at a concert by a Christian band
called the Sheep.

The Sheep were an American band who used to play
rock'n'roll covers of songs like 'O happy day'. It sounds
terrible now but I remember thinking they were pretty
good. At the end of the gig an evangelist spoke and
invited those of us who wanted to accept Jesus and go
to heaven to bow our heads and join in with a prayer. It
seemed like a fair offer to me, so I got my head down
and listened as this American evangelist geezer stood
behind me, shouting, 'Hallelujah! Praise the Lord!
You've given your life to Jesus.' I didn't feel that different
at the time, but it got me going along to church for a
few months. It didn't take long for my enthusiasm to

wear off, especially when being a Christian began to seem like such hard work. There were too many things going on in my life that took me further away from God, and after six months I had stopped going to church altogether. It was rebellion time.

Shortly after I had left school my parents moved to Wales, leaving me behind in Cheadle. I was 16, with my own place to live and a personal aim to lose the plot as much as possible. I tried absolutely everything, living the high life with what seemed like quite a decent wage I was bringing home as a cabinet-maker. I was convinced that I was having a good time, but God was on my case and he was answering Mum and Dad's prayers that had had them on their knees for years.

As well as praying hard for us, my mum tried her hand at a bit of practical evangelism, buying us a Christian book each year as one of our Christmas presents. As dutiful non-Christian sons we always ignored them, stuffing them under our beds or using them as firelighters. She always prayed that God would use the books to get through to us, and one year it paid off.

My brother Simon was going out with a girl called Lesley. One day she was looking around a second-hand bookshop when she saw a copy of a book called *Turned on to Jesus* by Arthur Blessitt. Because a friend had been telling her about Jesus, she paid the five pence required and took it home to read. She was so impressed with it that she gave it to Simon for him to read. He opened the book and inside the front cover were the words 'To

Simon, with love from Mum, Christmas 1972'. He recognised Mum's handwriting and immediately knew that this was the book Mum had bought him a few Christmases before. Even now no one is sure how the book got from his bedroom to the second-hand book-shop, into his girlfriend's hands and back round to him, but the whole thing had the mark of God all over it. It is just like the hound of heaven to go after Simon and not let him go. When Lesley gave him the book he soon began to realise that as well as being 'with love from Mum', it was also 'with love from God'. He read it with a passion, and just a few days later, while he was driving in his Bedford van, he gave his life to Jesus, saying that same prayer Dad had said 17 years earlier.

The Holy Spirit took over and Simon wept like a little baby. The next time I saw him I knew he was a different man: the purple hair and dreaded earring were still in place, but he was different. He was telling his friends and me that Jesus had completely changed his life and set him on fire. I was 17 years old and wanted to be a bit of a lad, so this kind of chat wasn't quite the sort of thing I was after, but he just kept on talking. I eventually gave in and agreed to go to church with him. It wasn't a particularly amazing service that we went to, but I remember coming out and thinking that it was a good thing I had just done. For the next six months I was pubbing and clubbing it in Manchester five or six nights and spending one night at church each week. Every time I went along I left feeling good about it, until one Sunday evening when Simon told his story in church.

He told the congregation exactly how he'd become a Christian and went through all the things that God had done for him. That night my heart melted, and I knew that I wanted to experience the same change that had happened to my brother, to get in touch with the power of Jesus. I went home and knelt by my bed. I can remember saying, 'God, I don't know if you're prepared to have me, but if you are I'm really going to go for it. I'm not going to stuff it up like I did when I was 12.' I wanted this to be different from what had happened after that Sheep concert. Whatever it cost, I was up for it.

I wasn't up to speed with the parable of the prodigal son, about how God welcomes people back, but in my bedroom I sensed that God was having me back and setting me on fire. I woke up the next morning feeling as if I wanted to talk to people about Jesus; feeling as if I wanted to read the Bible. I didn't speak in tongues but I believe God filled me with his Spirit and gave me the gift and the heart of an evangelist. In many ways it is precisely that which has kept me going these last 20-odd years of being a Christian: a passion for seeing people who don't know Jesus find him for themselves. Once I'd got up from beside my bed, Simon and I spent the next few months going around the pubs in Cheadle telling everybody we knew about Jesus, and spending ages each day reading the Bible and praying. We even got hold of some cheesy beer mats that said 'Come to your local . . . church!' to place strategically in front of the boozers. We were so fired up for Jesus that our lives had undergone a massive change.

Shortly after I became a Christian my mum and I went to the Keswick Bible Convention. I was blown away by this massive throng of 5,000 Christians all meeting under a huge banner that read 'All One in Christ Jesus'. After one of these meetings my mum introduced me to an old lady whose name was Olive Clarke.

'Ah,' she said, 'so you're Andrew. I've been praying for you every week for the past 17 years. Do you know Jesus?'

Stunned, I told her that I did.

'And your brothers, Simon and Michael, I've been praying for them too. Do they know Jesus?'

Even more stunned I told her that, yes, Jesus had turned them both around. I told Olive that one by one all of us Hawthorne boys had become Christians and that God was blessing the family so much. She was blown away too, and I'll never forget her telling me about how she had prayed for her own father every day of her Christian life. It wasn't until he was 87 years old that the stubborn old thing finally became a Christian himself.

When you get to heaven, you will notice a gigantic mansion with an immense garden. That will be the home of Mrs Olive Clarke, the wonderful saint. That lady's faithful prayers are one of the reasons that I am a Christian today, despite the fact she had never met me. I am also sure that God loves to work in family units; he hears our prayers for our family and stores them up; he knows how we feel about our mums and dads, brothers and sisters who aren't yet Christians. Right through the Bible God loves to save entire families and tribes. Even if they don't respond till they are on their death bed, it is worth praying those prayers, crying out to God to save the people we love the most. It seems clear to me that one of the great joys of getting into heaven is going to be the surprise of seeing the different people who were saved at the eleventh hour. I remember talking to Eric Delve – who is now a vicar – and he told me that he had never been with anybody on their deathbed who wasn't ready to pray and ask Jesus into their lives. It's my guess that there will be many of our families with us for all eternity who don't deserve to be there, who haven't lived for Jesus, but who are there by the grace of God. Surely it is worth our while praying those prayers even when it seems like a lost cause?

When I became a Christian, Cheadle was in the middle of the closest thing to revival that anyone there had ever seen. The local youth group started growing at an outrageous rate, going from being just a handful of young people to the largest Church of England youth group in Britain. It took just over a year for the numbers to reach a couple of hundred, and by that time a much needed new curate had arrived. Wally Benn is now an esteemed bishop, but back then he hadn't much experience of youth work and felt completely out of his depth. He decided to do the only sensible thing, and spent plenty of time each week locked away in his flat. Thankfully he wasn't hiding, but praying that God would do something. He pleaded with God to show him how to lead this mass of new Christians, and God took notice.

At that time my brother had joined a Christian punk rock band – the Bill Mason Band. They and others started going around local schools, helping to bring in all these fresh Christians. It was fantastic, and it was probably at that time that I caught the bug for schools work myself. It was obvious that there was a massive mission field on our own doorstep.

In the schools and colleges of Manchester an increasingly pagan generation was growing up without any real understanding of even the most basic elements of Christianity. It's got to be said that as a nation we have forgotten about God for almost 60 years since the Second World War. It's payback time now, and the price is rising levels of family breakdown, crime, suicide and many other social problems. What could be more rewarding and exciting than committing your life to changing this situation? By working and praying towards individuals being brought back to God, by expecting to be part of a whole nation's return to the Creator, you are signing up for the most rewarding and dangerous work out there.

These were some of the basics that we learnt back then. When we started to think, talk and pray about the church, it became clear that as an institution, the church has failed to understand what it is there for. We have the Master's instructions, which are not that hard to understand. I mean, there are some biblical statements that just could not be any clearer. Try this one for size: 'You are the light of the world. Don't take your light and put it under a bowl. Instead, put it on a stand.' The trouble is that no matter how clear the instructions seem to be, we have constantly disobeyed them. We've put our light under a bowl, or in other words we've got so caught up in the business of church buildings and church meetings that we've lost our way. If anyone lets in the light through our once-a-year sorties out into the darkness, we get them back under the bowl as quickly as possible. Surely this is not the way it's meant to be? The main purpose is not to be a cosy club for the few who have jumped through enough hoops and learnt enough of the jargon to call it home; the church is for out there. The church is meant to be what C. T. Studd called a 'rescue shop', going to a hurting world with the unimaginably good news of Jesus. What's more, the church needs to make sure that the way it communicates makes sense to the people it tries to reach. Accessibility and interaction should be a total priority of every Bible-believing church. Of course, at the very top of our agenda needs to be the issue of how we stay faithful to the age-old truths of Christianity, but our methods of sharing those truths with others should be a close second.

So how do we do it? No matter how great the coming revival is, it's fairly unlikely that people are going to come knocking on our church doors saying, 'What must I do to be saved?' We have to go out there in the power of the Holy Spirit, just like Peter and the boys did way back in the years of bread and sandals, and in the same way that radical believers have been doing ever since.

If we are really called to go where the people are, what better place to go to than the schools? It has amazed us all how open the schools are to us going in and working with their pupils. It even seems to be getting easier, just as long as you aren't a dribbling fanatic who tries to raise the dead in assemblies and have appeals just before double maths. The doors are wide open, and rightly so. We Christians should be allowed to go and teach what the Bible says and explain to people what the world's biggest religion is all about. I believe that many more Christians should be praying and trying to get into their local schools to help them teach about Jesus Christ. After all, He is the central figure of human history, and the Bible is the most amazing book ever written. What's the point of having religious education if we haven't got the believers to teach it? These are the arguments that the Tribe have used for the last 11 years, and it's the same bug I caught in 1978, as a fresh-faced 18-year-old excuse for an evangelist.

2

Pleasure and Pain

I'm worried that I might be looking at the past through rose-tinted spectacles, but as I think about those early years of being a Christian, all I can remember is a time of total blessing. As if meeting Jesus wasn't enough, I also had my eye on Michele Jones, a hot-looking 15-year-old who had become a Christian at one of my brother's gigs with the Bill Mason Band. Despite the fact that I was the 18-year-old youth leader, I knew I had to get in there, and sure enough I did. She became the love of my life and we married five years later.

More good things were happening for me at work. While it meant quitting the first job that I had ever really enjoyed – selling melamine-faced chipboard for kitchens – I started working with Simon in the business that he'd set up a year earlier. We sold leather crafts, fashion belts and all that kind of stuff. It also meant that I had loads of opportunities to be doing bits of evangelism on the side.

Several opportunities came my way during those years for me to go into full-time Christian work. At one point I even thought about becoming an Anglican vicar, but it never fell into place (in hindsight I think I would have made a disastrous vicar) so I carried on working with Simon. We were working hard at building up the business, and over time we moved out of the leather crafts market (hand-stitched tool-belts never did seem that cool), and into the world of fashion. We might not have had offices in Paris, Milan or London (Longsight Industrial Estate was more our style), but we were doing pretty well selling to high-street stores. Back then all the staff were Christians, and each day kicked off with a prayer time on the factory floor. As things got bigger we ran out of Christians and thought it might be a good thing if we took a few lads on from the job centre. The daily prayer meetings carried on the same, although this time there were a few blokes staring around, worrying that they had ended up in an asylum.

In the early 1980s Lady Diana arrived on the scene and set off a series of chain reactions that affected the whole nation. It seemed that whatever she wore became an instant hit and, because she was into accessories at the time, that was good news for businesses like ours. I don't remember exactly how it happened, but she might have gone out one night wearing a pair of men's braces. By the following Monday morning just about every young girl in Britain had to have their own pair of Lady Di braces. We had one little machine to make them, and soon found ourselves with orders for almost a million pairs.

We were desperate for help, so we went back to the job centre to see what they could do. We managed to get hold of a few more machines, and by the next day we were opening our doors to the biggest bunch of reprobates we had ever seen. We had no idea what a recruitment policy was, and the job centre had taken us at our word when we told them to send anybody who was prepared to work hard. What we got were all the lads who had just come out of Strangeways Prison or who had got sacked by every other employer in the area. There were some real nutters among them, and they brought with them all kinds of problems; from graffiti and vandalism to violence and theft. But what really bothered me and Simon was not just that they were wrecking our factory and not making a lot of braces, but that as we got to know them it became obvious the lads knew absolutely nothing about Jesus. In that respect they probably weren't much different from most young people in Britain today. They had no understanding of the cross, the resurrection or the need for a personal relationship with Jesus. For them Jesus was just another way of swearing.

One day Simon and I were sat at the 1987 Harrogate Fashion Fair trying to work out how we could present our faith to them. We were talking about how hopeless the church was at trying to reach this kind of guy with the gospel. We spent all afternoon coming up with increasingly crazy ideas. Eventually we got to the point of imagining someone getting all the churches in

Manchester to work together in supporting an event that would reach the city's toughest areas. It would need to be something pretty big, so we guessed that we'd have to take over the most credible rock venue in the area, which at that time was the 3,000-capacity Apollo Theatre, just down the road from our factory. Because we were in that kind of mood we decided that it would be too dull just to book it for one night, so instead we reckoned that it would be best if we had it for a whole week.

We were on a roll, and chatted for ages about how fantastic it would be if we could stuff that week full of credible evangelism that made sense to teenagers. We weren't talking about the normal cringe-making stuff that the church put on, but a series of events of such quality that thousands of people would be blown away. We spent all afternoon working on these dreams, and towards the end it felt as if God's finger was pointing down at us, encouraging us to have a go. It didn't take long for these 'what if?' suggestions to become 'why not?' decisions. We decided to go ahead and book the venue as well as write to all the churches in Manchester to try to get them behind us. Later that day as we drove home it felt as though my car was floating six inches above the road. I felt so excited; I was sure that God had spoken, and that despite the fact I was an unknown youth group evangelist who made braces, my brother and I were about to do something mad for Him.

I went home that night and spoke to my long-time confidant and friend, Val Grieve. When I had finished telling him of the plans he suggested that I went round to see him the next day. I sat in bed that night and opened my Bible, ready to tackle that day's reading from my *Bible in One Year*. I was up to Isaiah 43, and before I read it I asked God that if our plan was from Him, He would give me some sort of encouragement from the Bible over the next days. Looking back I wish I had had the bottle to ask Him to speak to me right then, but God knew what He was doing. I believe that out of all the verses in the Bible, those found in Isaiah 43 were the very best ones I could have read that night. As I started reading them they seemed to jump right out at me. Verse 5 told me to 'not be afraid, for I am with you; I will bring your children from the east and gather you from the west. I will say to the north, "Give them up!" and to the south, "Do not hold them back."' Then came verse 10, where it says, '"You are my witnesses," declares the Lord, "my servant whom I have chosen."' And when I had finished reading verse 19 I was utterly stunned.

'See,' said the prophet, 'I am doing a new thing! Now it springs up; do you not perceive it? I am making a way in the desert and streams in the wasteland. The wild animals honour me, the jackals and the owls, because I provide water in the desert and streams in the wasteland, to give drink to my people, my chosen, the people I formed for myself that they may proclaim my praise.'

I put my Bible down, convinced that God had spoken to

me. I phoned Simon up and read him the verses too. Weird as it seemed at the time, it was clear that God had picked a couple of divvies like us for this purpose, and that He was going to do a new thing through it. All that stuff about seeing a way in the desert and streams in the wasteland was the direct answer to the things we had been praying for. Some of those nutters we had taken on at the factory definitely fitted the 'wild animal' description, and to think that they would soon be meeting and praising God was a dream come true.

When we met with Val Grieve, he told us that the next day he was going to a meeting of the key church leaders in Manchester. He invited us along, and to help turn on the charm, Simon and I decided to turn up wearing our best suits. We later found out that we looked like a couple of drug dealers, but the assorted vicars and pastors were kind enough not to mention it. Instead they listened to us asking for their support. We told them that if they were prepared to support us and set up some serious missions, then we would take the risk and book the Apollo Theatre for a week. These church leaders had never met us before, but to our amazement they all agreed that the idea seemed to be one of God's. With them behind us we booked the Apollo right away, wrote to all the churches and took a guy on to help us administrate the whole thing.

What followed a year later was amazing. In the run-up to the big week there were 300 local missions, which all helped pull in over 20,000 young people to the event that we called the Message '88. For seven nights we stuffed the place full of performers like Gloria Gaynor, Paul Jones and Mike Peters from the Alarm. We had loads of Christian bands who were hip at the time, like Heartbeat, Triumph and a couple of lads in a pop combo that called itself Except for Access.

So many good things happened, but at the end of it we were exhausted. We had spent a year working on it, and we were shocked to find out that someone had declared braces un-cool again. Simon and I both knew that the business needed lots of work put into it, especially as we had started the Message with a budget of about £60,000, but as time had gone by and more opportunities and expenses came along, the budget had gone up to £100,000. God had brought all of it in wonderfully, apart from about £6,000. As the business had slowed down, this was not good news, and we spent three months trying to sort things out. The Apollo were understandably starting to get a bit stressed about their cash, but our overdraft was at the maximum and that six grand seemed a long way off. As I sat in our office in Longsight, I asked God what was going on. If I was sure that God was in it before, now the event had been and gone I was absolutely positive; so many good things had come out of it that the whole thing had God's signature plastered all over it. Plenty of people had become Christians and loads of ministries had sprung up. How could it be that we were skint and in debt to the venue? I asked God to step in one more time and provide the cash, but driving home that night I felt tired and low. The phone rang as soon as I walked through the door.

'Hello,' said the voice at the other end of the line. 'I'm an 87-year-old lady and I would like to give you some money.'

I can remember thinking that I was a 28-year-old man who would certainly like to get my hands on some of her money. She told me how she had invested in an investment package that had gone bad. Along with many others she had lost all her savings, and it had been years before she got any back. By this time she had told God that since she had no need for it, she would let Him have it. She then told me that she planned on putting a cheque for £3,000 in the post that night. To say this encouraged me was an understatement, and as she told me where she lived I went round straight away with a bunch of flowers. As well as being polite, somewhere in the back of my mind was the hope that she might give me the cheque there and then.

Walking into her house was like walking into the presence of God. She was an awesome old lady, another Olive Clarke, and as we started to pray together she put on a head covering and cried out passionately to God for the young people of Manchester. My cunning plan had a double pay-off: not only did she give me the cheque that night, but she gave more than she said, making it out for £4,000. I hoped it wasn't a mistake and paid it in as soon as the bank opened the next day.

Within hours we had another surprise. A VAT return arrived in the post, and we suddenly had enough money to settle up all the accounts for the Message '88. It was as if God had said that He was behind it all, but that He wanted us to learn to have faith and to believe that when He calls us to do something then He will provide. That has pretty much been the story of our last 15 years; God has stepped in with some wild provisions, but so often it seems that He leaves it till the last minute. We have never had much money in the bank, but every time we have taken a risk on something that we have believed God was into, He has always provided.

It seems to me that there is a link that exists between ministries of vision and small bank balances. I know loads of people who are fired up with big ideas about things they can do for God, but who have very little cash. People of vision, people of passion who want to see things get done simply cannot stand to sit on loads of money. I know when I look at £1,000 I like to think that I don't see security; I see a wage for someone working in the inner city. In my experience, churches who live off their interest are nearly always dying out. From the start we've always tried to be a ministry that lives on the edge. This means that when it comes to virtually every pay day I'm asking God when the money's going to appear. Each time God turns up. Over the years our budgets have increased, but God has always been incredibly faithful. However, this way of living can be hard work. Recently, as we approached another pay day, wondering where on earth the money was going to come from, I started complaining to a friend of mine called Nick. I said that month after month getting the team to cry out to God for their salaries was wearing.

How nice it would be just to have a breather for a few months and focus our energies on something else.

Nick has had experience of this kind of thing before. For years he worked on the Operation Mobilisation ship *Doulos*, where similarly, month after month and port after port, they, as a team, would have to rely on God's blessing. That experience has left him with plenty of wisdom, and his reply made perfect sense: 'Wearing? What do you think it's wearing?' he said. 'Probably your self-sufficiency and independence and any belief that you can provide the money through your own efforts and contacts. Anything that gets you to a place of total dependency and makes you pray more has got to be a blessing.'

Getting back to the story, after the close call of the Message '88 Simon and I decided to get seriously stuck into our business. Some of the church leaders had other ideas, and they came to see us to talk about putting on the Christmas Message '89. They felt things were on a roll, and that to stop now would be foolish. So, nervously, we agreed. We took on another person to travel around the churches to get them fired up about putting on missions. As the missions happened through-out the year the sense of excitement mounted. At the same time things got steadily worse for the business. On the morning of 21 December 1989 Simon and I sat in the liquidator's office, signing away a business that had finally gone bust. Later that evening I was preaching the gospel to nearly 3,000 young people at the Manchester Apollo. It was a confusing day. I remember asking God what was going on. I had tried to be a good boy, I'd tried to be faithful and do the mission for him, yet there I was with a bankrupt business on my hands. I spent sleepless nights asking God why. I couldn't see why we had ended up with all this debt and aggravation when we felt we'd tried our best to be two faithful, hardworking boys. It just didn't add up.

Then I learnt a lesson. If you think of it as a coin, then God's provision has a flip-side. In the midst of the euphoria of my youth – the falling in love and getting married, seeing the business grow and watching all the exciting things that were happening around me – I had missed out on this valuable lesson. Christianity isn't a cop-out, it isn't a bypass of life's problems; Christians do have businesses that go bust, they do get cancer, they do have family members that die and they will have horrible things happen to them. Sometimes God will step in and sort it out in an instant; He can heal people and He can restore businesses and pour piles of money and orders in if He wants to. But at other times God can be the one who pulls the plug, teaching us lessons that we will only take on board once He has our full attention. What Christianity is, though, is a way through life's problems, providing everyone with the power to go through them. That Christmas God had me sat down in the classroom, making sure I learnt that lesson. I am sure that He was also giving me a new desire to go into full-time Christian work, and yet early on in 1990 Simon and I committed ourselves one last time to resurrecting the business. We were determined not to be sidetracked, but to get on with trying to sell bum bags, braces and belts and any other daft stuff we could shift. My mate Mark Pennells had other ideas.

Mark had played at one of the Apollo gigs in 1988 in the band Except for Access. Like many of us he had been amazed by the things he had seen God do at the time. He'd been working more and more in schools with his band, and he now found himself with a fresh passion for getting out there and reaching the people who needed God the most. He came to see Simon and me with an idea for something he wanted to call 'Message to Schools'.

Years later I remember sitting in a World Wide Message Tribe prayer meeting when God spoke to me through that classic verse in Romans 8 where it says, 'We know that in all things God works for the good of those who love him' (v. 28). Right down the centuries Christians have twisted those words to mean that God will turn every situation around for good, even the tough things. For example, if a business goes bust, then there will soon be another one along that will make even more money. The theft of a Ford Escort should really be a cue for rejoicing at the imminent arrival of a brand new VW Golf. If our girlfriend decided to dump us, then surely it can't be long before that page-3 stunner comes bouncing round the corner. All things working together for good? Rubbish! What the Bible goes on to say in the two verses that follow is this: 'For those God foreknew he also predestined to be conformed to the likeness of his Son, that he might be the firstborn among many brothers and sisters.'

In other words, the good that God is going to bring out of all things is that we will become more like Jesus. That may mean going through some tough things, but the truth is that we cannot ignore this reality. If we want to become more like Jesus with each day that passes, we need to trust God. If we do, then even the most horrific experiences will help with the job of transforming us 'into his likeness from one degree of glory to another' (2 Corinthians 3:18, RSV). The big questions that face us all are: Are we doing that? Are we being transformed from one degree of glory into another? Are we being transformed into His likeness with ever-increasing glory? Am I more glorious as a Christian, more like Jesus today, than I was yesterday? Am I far, far more glorious than I was a year ago? How much do I resemble His Son? *That*, I believe, is what God wants to do through all the trials, the problems and the difficulties of life; to shape and mould us, to put us through the fire sometimes, but only so that we can come out purer and more like His Son, who becomes easier to spot in us.

3

The Birth of the Music

Since leaving Huddersfield University, Mark Pennells and Zarc Porter had spent six years in a band called Except for Access. They had met while studying for their music degrees, and were both Christians with the big aim of breaking into the charts. Instead of six years of glamour, however, they went through six years of frustration as they travelled to dozens of meetings with record labels, all the time getting nowhere. Plenty of these big label people showed an interest, but after nothing happened, the boys realised that they were continually being 'bottom-drawered'; placed away for safe-keeping along with all the other acts that there wasn't quite enough confidence to release. By keeping them down in the drawer at least the labels knew that they could still make a bit of cash should the band develop a bit of a buzz or happen to write a killer song. There are so many people – in fact I would say so many brilliantly talented Christian musicians – who waste their lives by chasing record deals and elusive hits. Even if they do make it, more often than not all they end up with is 15 minutes of fame and a swift transfer to the bargain bin.

Mark and Zarc visited them all, and one time were sitting in the offices of Bill Latham, Cliff Richard's manager. In bounced Cliff in his tennis gear and Bill introduced them by telling Cliff that here were two young lads trying to break into the music business. 'Hi,' said Cliff. 'Aren't we all!' before running off for his game of tennis.

That seemed to be the story of those years: endless visits but no success. They were a good band and did some good gigs. They tried to be evangelistic, and often I would be preaching with them as they did it, but there was a general sense that too much time had been wasted that could have been used otherwise. This all came to a head for Mark and Zarc during 1988 and 1989. The band had been doing more schools work (which seemed like a fantastic opportunity), plus they'd played at the two Message gigs which had seemed so credible and where so many young people were becoming Christians. Mark in particular got a real desire to evangelise. Even though he didn't feel like much of a preacher, his heart was totally up for seeing young people get to know Jesus.

As Simon and I chatted with Mark, we listened to him describing his frustration at trying to break into the secular music scene. Zarc was working nights in a garage in order to help fund the setting up of his new recording studio (Perfect Music), and Mark was absolutely skint. We weren't doing too well ourselves, but Simon and I thought that they were both talented, and we agreed to do what we could. We contacted some other businessmen and Mark chatted with some of his friends. Over the next few months between us we raised £7,000 to get Mark on the road.

Since the first time we met it had been obvious that Mark and I were going to get on well. When Simon and I agreed to help Mark and Zarc out in 1991, the two of us spent quite a bit of time together, talking through the many possibilities that lay ahead. We both agreed on schools as the main focus for Mark's work, and soon began to lay down some basic principles that might help keep us on the straight and narrow. We thought we were setting up a project that might run for a couple of years; we never guessed that it would last for so long and grow so big. Still, the principles must have worked, and they've been at the heart of everything we've done ever since.

The first principle that we knew we had to adopt was the belief that Manchester would be our primary focus. There were enough young people in the area to keep us going for a lifetime, and besides, Mark had had quite enough of travelling all over the country doing gigs he couldn't stand, being fed nothing but cold quiche and vol-au-vents.

The second principle I wanted to put in place was the word of God: we wanted the Bible to be at the heart of everything. From the start Mark and I agreed to spend more time preaching and teaching the Bible than doing the pop tunes that Mark was going to sing. As before, this was something different, and we knew that if we didn't get things sorted at the start, we would both end up working on something neither of us was totally happy with.

Finally we decided that we should never lose sight of the fact that it was young non-Christians that we were working for. This went hand in hand with the decision to make Manchester our priority. We had seen too many churches pour valuable resources into misplaced projects. A staggering amount of the church's energy goes on the fat and healthy flock who are already saved and have no need of evangelistic messages. Those people are sorted and are going to heaven, so the church needs to get a different set of priorities. From the very beginning we made it clear that it was people who weren't Christians who would be receiving the bulk of our resources.

Looking back on it now, those principles have served us well. Sticking to a diet of Manchester, the Bible and the lost might not be the most exciting way of living, but keeping it simple has made it easier to avoid distractions.

There was one final principle we put in place back then which has served us well over the years. Having talked for ages with Mark about the way things often went wrong for other bands, we decided that all money earned through the band – the royalties for song-writing, radio play and all the rest – would be ploughed straight back into the ministry. This didn't mean that we would try and starve people; instead we opted for paying people wages. From then on we decided that no one would ever get rich, no matter how successful we became. The wages are set by the trustees, and these days the principle has been extended to include speaking fees and book royalties. Keeping our sticky little fingers away from the cash has meant that God has been entirely free to bless the work – something He seems to have been doing with frightening regularity.

Once we had hammered out these standards we were ready for our launch. A guy called Baz Gascoigne came down to preach at a service held at Mark's church in Cheadle Hulme. Midway through he pulled Mark up the front and gave him a prophecy.

'Mark,' he said, 'I really believe God is on this thing, and that you are going to be used not only in Manchester but also in Britain, Europe and the rest of the world. God is going to use you beyond your wildest dreams.'

After so much time spent working out that we *weren't* going to get distracted by plans to leave Manchester, this came as a bit of a shock. The church didn't exactly have a reputation for big-time prophecies, and Mark wasn't too impressed with this latest revelation. Still, as we have found out over time, God and Baz were right.

We decided not to worry too much about the future, and instead got on with the job of doing some schools work. We started in Cheadle Hulme, and did two secondary schools back to back. During the week, Mark was involved in assemblies and lunch-time meetings, while I tried to get away from the business as much as possible to join him. At the end of it all we put on a concert at Cheadle Hulme High School, in their largest assembly hall. On the night about 75 bored-looking kids turned up, spacing themselves out around the edges to make it look as if there were even fewer of them. While they looked bored, Mark and I looked petrified, seriously convinced that we were about to kick off our ministry with a massive flop. Eventually Mark got out there and did his stuff and I did my preaching, after which we invited anyone who was interested in receiving Jesus to go into the school changing rooms. Mark and I sat there waiting, hoping that we might score a result and get one or two walking through the door. Within minutes we were surrounded by 39 of them, all hungry for God. Mark and I looked at each other in total amazement, both thinking that it felt as if we had hit upon God's agenda. To have so many people respond at the end seemed like God's way of saying that He liked the cocktail of Manchester-Bible-lost. It was, to say the least, exciting.

Mark was writing his own material for the schools gigs, and was in the process of recording a tape of his pop tracks at the little studio that Zarc was setting up in his one-bedroomed flat down the road. By the summer of 1992 the rave scene was massive and all over the country were new bands and illegal parties. Zarc's studio was soon home to more dance-orientated sounds, and I used to love sitting in on their sessions. One day I booked some time in the studio to put some rap tracks down, despite the fact that I had never been a rapper or any kind of a musician. I thought it would be a bit of fun, and Mark and Zarc liked what came out. After that I began supporting Mark at gigs, doing two or three songs before he came on.

One day I was in the studio when Mark and Zarc were playing around with a harder type of music that Mark could work with. I had been reading a book about the Scottish Hebridean revival and I started telling them about it all. What had happened in 1949 was that a guy called Duncan Campbell had been summoned to preach on the island of Lewis by two old ladies, Peggy and Elizabeth Smith. One of them was 83 and the other was 87, and one had arthritis while the other was blind. They were devastated by the way things had changed on the island after the Second World War: where the churches had been full, they were now spewing out young people at an alarming rate. God was being replaced by alcohol. Peggy and Elizabeth were so moved by this that they cried out to God and called Duncan Campbell to preach the gospel to the island's young people.

Campbell had arrived and was attending regular prayer meetings with the dwindling church member-ship. One night, at three in the morning, their prayers were interrupted by the building shaking from the total chaos that was occurring outside the church. People were running out into the streets, repenting. Speaking later, Campbell said that in the days that followed it was hard to find anyone who wasn't seeking God. When I read those words I was so fired up that I couldn't stop talking about it. As I finished telling them in the studio, immediately Zarc started putting some tracks down, suggesting that we write a song about it. So within half an hour we had come up with 'Revival'; the result of our first time of working together.

We used this track in the live set, with me coming back for a guest slot after I had done my little support slot. The kids totally flipped, and again it felt as if we had really hit on something. The numbers at the gigs shot up and Mark's pop tape was hijacked by all these mad 'dancey' ideas. I had a bit of input, although it was limited to a few lyrics and ideas for songs and plenty of vocal encouragement to put more funny noises in. I liked those funny noises, and it was a great time of inspiration where we felt as if we were discovering a new platform for the gospel. It was over that summer that we decided to form a band, not just to have Mark doing his solo pop thing.

The inspiration for the band's name came from some other names that were around at the time. It seemed that every other rave act had the words 'massive' or 'tribe' in their name, and Simon and I had just finished embroidering some T-shirts that said 'Massive Global Technics Posse'. So I suggested that we call ourselves the 'Massive World Wide Message Tribe'. Most of my good ideas seem to get a little better once Mark and

Zarc have watered them down, so we ditched the 'Massive' part.

We found a singer called Elaine Hanley, who was fairly well known on the Manchester gospel scene. We also got another girl in to dance and sing with us. Lorraine Williams was a Salvation Army girl who had worked with Mark a few times before. Mark and I made the mistake of inviting Lorraine for a drink at our favourite pub and ordering a couple of pints. We were halfway through them when we realised that as a member of the Salvation Army she would have signed 'the pledge', and was sitting looking worried, quietly sipping her lemonade. Her joining the band was therefore a bit of a miracle.

It was about this time that Mark and Zarc dubbed me 'Heavyfoot'. I wasn't too keen, but I saw their point; every time I recorded a rap I used to get all excited and stamp my foot on the floor. It annoyed the neighbours so much that I ended up with a cushion underneath my foot. No matter how many times I explained it to my mum, though, she never quite got it, and worried it was something to do with wearing ill-fitting shoes as a child.

When we finally got around to releasing our first schools tape we all agreed not to put a lot of work into promoting it. *Take a Long Hike with the Chosen Few* had taken months to record, and getting out on the road would have taken us away from our Manchester schools, so we decided to sell it only in schools. There was another reason why we couldn't go out on big promotional trips, and that was because we had filled the diary with bookings for schools missions for nearly a whole year in advance. Something had happened, and without too much difficulty we were fully booked.

As we visited each school – taking assemblies, lessons and finishing off with a concert – we developed better relationships with the local churches. Over time we began to see a theme that was common to many of them: they were up for seeing God move and impact a generation, but they didn't all have the resources to disciple them. It was terrible to think of all these young kids getting a taste of Jesus, only to forget about it as all the other pressures of life overwhelmed their baby faith. It was after a couple of years of these missions that we were able to provide some follow-up material which we hoped would help. *Get God – the Video* was our first attempt. It was basic and cheap – made up of me mouthing off to the camera in a church hall in Cheadle – but it helped the churches hang on to their new recruits for a bit longer.

With *Take a Long Hike with the Chosen Few* recorded, we were putting all our energies into the missions, having almost forgotten about promoting the tape. Meanwhile, a guy called Steve Nixon, a DJ in Stoke, somehow got hold of a copy of the tape and wrote to us. He told us how he had recently been to see the Shamen in concert. At the time their gigs were almost like evangelistic New Age services, complete with a preacher and all sorts of stuff. The idea of the potential influence they could have really disturbed Steve, and he prayed that God would raise up an answer to the

Shamen – a Christian band to reach the dance music culture. It was the very next day that our tape landed on his doorstep. From then on he seemed to go on a one-man promotional campaign. We couldn't pay him, but he just felt fired up to spread the word about the band wherever he could. He sent it to his friend, a Christian producer in America called Scott Blackwell, who owned a label called N Soul. In Britain a buzz also started to develop, with more and more orders coming in for *Take a Long Hike*. Scott Blackwell heard it and contacted us, saying that he wanted to release it in the USA. He paid us a bit of money to add a few new tracks and, in 1993, our first CD hit the shops in America.

Meanwhile, back in Britain the word was travelling about these mad schools workers who never left Manchester. At first we were turning down little church gigs, with 50 or 60 kids, but the more the news spread, the bigger the gig offers became. For a while people called us 'the band you can't book' as we literally turned down anything that wasn't in front of Manchester school kids. Soon, we decided that this didn't necessarily have to be the case, and we started to spread our wings in the summer and Easter holidays. The priorities remained the same, but the opportunities to raise extra support were too good to be missed. Even to this day, each year begins with us booking up missions and making sure that they are prepared and followed up well. If there are any gaps left over then we fill them with whatever opportunities come along.

It was in the summers of 1993 and 1994 that we did

our first gigs outside Manchester. We did a few Christian festivals – a couple with the word 'cross' in their names (although that wasn't one of our criteria) – and played in front of our first large groups of Christians. The 1993 gig at Cross Rhythms seemed to go well, but it wasn't until the two that followed in the next summer that things took off. At one of the gigs in Liverpool, Gerald Coates was speaking, and I remember trying to get him to say something nice about our ministry so we could print it in our literature. Gerald meanwhile wasn't really taking much notice of my suggestion; instead he was homing in on Mark. Just before our biggest gig so far he told Mark that the next seven years would be very important in his life. He said that he thought God was going to use Mark way beyond his wildest dreams, and that God was on him and the ministry. Mark was understandably blown away by this, but we didn't have to wait long for some sort of confirmation, as the crowd seemed to love the gig, and mobbed the stall later, buying up loads of copies of *Take a Long Hike*. While we knew the stuff went down well with our Manchester school kids, the nice Christians in the UK might have reacted differently. Thankfully they didn't, and things moved on.

As we got over the gig, we had a call from one of the promoters of a large Christian music festival in Holland called FLEVO. One of their main acts had dropped out, and with just three days to go, they needed to come up with a band that the 10,000-strong crowd would be into, as well as all the other people who would be watching it on national television. We were probably the least qualified band in the world to do this, but they sounded desperate, so we gave it a go. We turned up looking like a particularly scraggy bunch of schools workers, and stared in amazement at the set-up. The stage was huge, the lighting rig looked as if it would need half the national grid to power it and the video wall was straight out of the next century.

By the time we were due on stage we had stopped staring and got down to the business of being seriously worried; FLEVO was a pretty standard Christian rock festival, and we churned out pretty non-standard Christian dance music. It all could have gone so wrong, but in the end it all went right. They had had enough of listening to older people tell them how dance music was of the devil, and how one five-minute dose of S-express was enough to damn your soul for all eternity. They were absolutely gagging for it. We attended a press conference afterwards where, for the first time ever, we were talked of as 'pop stars' and even 'musicians'. Both sounded funny at the time, but if you are not careful, no matter how focused you are, that stuff can turn your head. It was a lot of fun, but in some ways it was good to get back to Manchester and into the schools, remembering what we were all about.

It was around this time that we had our first approach from a UK record label. We met up with Dave Bruce, the A and R man from Alliance Music. They were interested in releasing *Take a Long Hike* in the UK, or at least they were until we explained our vision and how we wouldn't be able to do anything during term-time. He went away to think about it and wrote back shortly afterwards saying that they liked the stuff but that because of our restrictions they couldn't see how it could work out. We still have the letter somewhere, and pull it out whenever we want to make them feel bad. Today Alliance are our record company, but only after some strange things happened. First, once Scott Blackwell had released the CD in America and the rest of his N Soul material was doing well, Alliance started distributing most of his releases over here. They ended up putting out *Take a Long Hike* on Alliance over here and despite the fact that we were hardly ever able to go out and promote it, it sold well enough for them to sign us anyway.

While this talk of transatlantic record deals and decent sales sounds nice, I was struggling about work. I could not decide whether to go full time with the band or not. I was spending all of my spare time doing ministry stuff – going out with the Tribe, being one of the trustees (we had finally become a charitable trust) and working on the wider vision for the band – yet I also had a commitment to Simon. In many ways he was the brains behind the business and I was the mouth, the one who went out on the road to bring in the orders. There were now a lot of mouths to feed, and it was all getting to be a bit of a struggle.

The strain showed itself in funny ways at first. I am well known for getting people's names wrong, espe-cially when I am stressed. On one particular occasion we were doing the last assembly of the week in front of the whole of Hattersley High School. I was supposed to thank the head of RE – a lovely Christian man called Mr Ryder – and the headteacher, Mr Leyland. Mark could see that my head was in a state, so he told me to think of Knight Rider. I went onto the platform muttering under my breath, 'Knight Rider, Knight Rider, Knight Rider . . .' When it came round to my speech, I confidently blurted out, 'We'd like to say a big thank you to Mr Knight, your RE teacher.' Obviously the pupils all loved this. As they started laughing I realised my mistake, but made it worse by thanking their head-master, Mr Hattersley.

At another school (this time safely away in Macclesfield) I was introduced to their new head of RE who, unlike their old one, was young, shapely and attractive. Again I was running late as I was introduced to this young woman wearing a tight top and mini skirt. For some reason, as I said 'H-h-hello', a globule of spit shot out of my mouth and onto the end of her nose. We then had an incredibly embarrassing five-minute conversation where neither of us would own up to the offending spittle while Mark was creased up behind the assembly hall curtain.

But giving up on the business would mean some-thing more serious than me having a better memory and less spit. Michele and I now had a couple of chil-dren and a 400-year-old cottage. Life was definitely busy, but we had a nice lifestyle to go with it. Along with the other trustees I had set Mark's wage some time before, and I knew that if I joined I would be on the same pay. Understandably Michele was stressed about the idea of moving from that beautiful house, especially as we thought the alternative would be a tiny two-bedroomed terrace. But it was clear that God was on our case and that He was leading both us and our family into full-time Christian work.

Before we had made up our minds though, we talked it through with our vicar, Donald Alistair. He was thrilled with the idea but said that it needed to be Michele's decision even more than mine as it was going to be a lot harder for her. She would be the one left at home while I would be charging around with all my exciting ministry stuff. This was wise advice but it also put even more pressure on Michele. However, at around the same time she got an amazing letter from Jane, a long-lost friend in Canada, who urged us to go into full-time ministry despite the fact that she knew nothing about our situation.

At the time there weren't any prophetic words or scriptures coming my way, but everything seemed to point to the conclusion that God was in it and that going full time would be the right decision to make. In my experience that is what most guidance is like: God speaking through the practical. So often we get stressed about things in life like which university we should go to, which person we should go out with or which church we should be involved in, all the time making things more complicated than they need to be. I believe that if we keep our eyes on Jesus we will know the answer to these questions, and even if they don't seem obvious, our lives will follow God's course. If you're looking for the classic verses on this you should turn to Romans 12, where Paul writes:

> I urge you, brothers and sisters, in view of God's mercy, to offer your bodies as living sacrifices, holy and pleasing to God – this is your spiritual act of worship. Do not conform any longer to the pattern of this world, but be transformed by the renewing of your mind. Then you will be able to test and approve what God's will is – his good, pleasing and perfect will.

According to Paul, if we are prepared to present our bodies as living sacrifices, to pay the price of really committing our lives to Christ and being prepared not to be directed by the world's standards, but to let the Spirit renew us and our minds, then we will know what God's will is. Guidance won't be a source of stress and worry; instead it will become part of our trust, faith and everyday expectations.

Another reason for changing the way I was working was the amount of pressure I was putting on our marriage. I was working hard in the business but even harder with the ministry. Stupidly, I thought I was being incredibly spiritual by being out almost every night doing 'the ministry stuff'. There are so many Christian workers who are no different from the businessmen I used to know; they are full of bravado about the outrageous number of hours they work, being out all day and getting home knackered. While they may be doing it under the assumption that it's all very spiritual, the truly spiritual thing is to go home and put your kids to bed. In fact the hardest thing for me has been putting the Message down at 5.30 each night and going home to be with my family.

As far as I'm concerned, there can be no doubt that I made the right decision back then. Not only was it right for me and my marriage, but it also turned out well for Simon's business. After a tough time at first, my leaving was the best thing that ever happened to the business. It turned out that I was its biggest overhead, and after I left, Simon ended up making more money than ever, making sure that plenty of it went to support the Message Trust. Of course there have been times when it would have been nice to have been earning a big wad in the business community, but over the last few years it has been my joy and privilege to be able to think full time about nothing else but kingdom things. I have been able to focus all my energies on building up this ministry and working for revival among Manchester's young people. It has been the most exciting part of my whole life and I am so glad that in 1993 I was able to burn my bridges and go full time with what was then called the Message to Schools Trust.

4

From Demo to Limo

Throughout 1994 the work we did in schools developed. We began to provide the schools with a better, more complete service, and the news about what we were doing continued to spread throughout Manchester. We were also learning to look at our job not just as a series of lessons and gigs, but as a responsibility to follow up the young people themselves alongside their local churches. On top of this, things were ticking over nicely in the States, and after our first two non-schools gigs the previous summer, the requests were flying in.

But still the full-time staff only consisted of myself and Mark, joined a few months later by Rob Ruston, who faithfully took on all the jobs that I'm hopeless at, such as the admin and technical stuff. Us two lads would go into school in the mornings, leading assemblies for the whole school, one year at a time. We would also do RE lessons with as many young people as possible, as well as lunch-time concerts whenever we could. By Friday night we would involve the rest of the band and any friends and volunteers who were interested to help pull off an evangelistic concert. Almost always God would turn up big time at these gigs, despite the fact that the crowd were often a bit on the lively side. It often seemed like total chaos during the music, with between a third and a half of the school turning up and jumping, dancing and making loads of noise. During those times I would be praying desperately. Somehow, when it came time for my preaching slot, there would normally be absolute silence and a real sense of God's presence. It became quite usual to see between 40 and 50 young people commit their lives to Christ on a night, and in general those gigs felt as though they had God's mark on them.

I say 'in general', for there were one or two exceptions. In some of the rougher schools there have been fights going on while I've been preaching. At least once or twice it has seemed that the vast majority of the audience were passionately snogging during my attempts to deliver the gospel. There was one terrible time when, because we couldn't do the concert in school, we held it in a local youth club. It was a weird place, the kind where kids were encouraged to draw pictures of gay parents and stick them up on the wall alongside condom adverts and pictures of topless women. The local church had been praying around every room during the day, and as we arrived it almost seemed as if something had been stirred up, but the job had not quite been finished. The concert was terrible and the kids literally started a riot. At first they were running through our dressing-room, nicking all our things and fighting with each other. While one girl was having an epileptic fit, for some reason the rest of the kids were outside trying to smash the door down. Eventually the police turned up to calm it all down, but the kids started a fight with them. To put it mildly, it didn't go down as one of our better gigs. Thankfully that sort of gig has been the exception, and I'm sure that if God hadn't been so on our side it would have been a very different story.

As the weeks passed we saw more and more people becoming Christians, and we tried to work in areas where the local churches could provide discipleship support once we had been and gone. This all sounded fine, until we realised that we were spending less time where our heart lay: the inner city. We always felt that that was our thing – the rivers in the desert and streams in the wasteland – but it was so hard to find churches in the inner city with any sort of developed youth work. In the few places where we had been, the new Christians would only last a few months. Inevitably we found ourselves getting drawn out into the suburbs and into the domain of the lively churches.

While this was on our minds, things were hotting up in America. Scott Blackwell was working hard, first of all pushing *Take a Long Hike* and then, in 1994, getting behind our second recording, *Dance Planet*. This was a project we had been working on during the summer of

1993, and had started selling in the schools. Scott liked it and decided to release it and a couple of singles. Quickly we learnt that the American singles market was very different from our own, and that instead of being on sale for just a few weeks, it meant getting it played on the radio for as many months as possible. Although the majority of the hundreds of Christian stations across the country churned out an extremely cheesy and wet blend of music, there was a little room for dance music. Scott released two tracks called 'Make it happen' and 'Short life', which have to go down as two of the worst songs we or anyone else has ever written. They were both kind of wimpy, but that didn't seem to matter, as they did pretty well on the Christian Hit Radio (CHR) chart. Scott finally got round to releasing what we thought was a decent track – one we had recorded in the autumn called 'I'm on my way to Zion' – and it reached number one in the charts. I think it was the first time a British Christian band had ever done that, which all helped the buzz to grow a little bit more.

Several of the big American Christian labels started to express an interest, and we found ourselves being approached by a variety of big men in nice suits, who all seemed to want us to use them to distribute the next album. Warner Alliance were the Christian division of Warner Brothers, the biggest media corporation in the world. Their people came over to talk to our people (Mark, me and Zarc) about all the possibilities they thought lay ahead. Again we gave them the spiel about how tough Manchester school kids came first and how travel would only be possible for a couple of weeks each year. This didn't seem to be too much of a hurdle for them, and in fact I got the impression that they kind of liked it. Because of the size (and turnover) of the American Christian scene it can be easy for artists to go off the rails and wind up being totally into a life of excess. Warner Alliance had had some first-hand experience of this not long before we met, when their main artist, the day after winning no fewer than seven DOVE awards, had a very public 'fall'. His double life caught up with him and Warner could do nothing but drop him.

When we arrived and started going on about how we put Manchester before money, I think Warner Alliance saw it as an opportunity to put their weight behind something they truly believed in. They even talked about distributing our *Get God* discipleship video to 10,000 youth leaders across America, as well as all sorts of other great plans. This impressed us as it wasn't really going to benefit them a great deal in terms of record sales, but it would help to sell our vision for the schools of Manchester. We liked it a lot and signed up.

All these negotiations took a long time, and it was the autumn of 1995 by the time the deal was in place and we could give them any material to release. At the start of the summer we had been working frantically to finish off our third full-length album, *We Don't Get What We Deserve*. When I say 'we', it had mainly been Zarc who was held hostage in the studio for the whole of June. He emerged at the end with a fine album, but a dishevelled look that earned him the name 'Swamp Thing'.

Alliance got on with the business of distributing the new album in the UK in time for the new school year in September. Their American cousins were not due to release it for a while, but they were desperate for us to go over to the States to join in the fun and help with the promotions. We were fully booked with schools missions, but managed to squeeze in one six-day and one four-day trip either side of a schools mission at Blessed Thomas Halford School in Altrincham. On one of these trips we visited a booksellers' convention in Los Angeles. Not knowing what to expect, Sophie (one of our new dancers) and I were surprised when we turned up to find thousands of booksellers from all over the world gathering together to sell anything and everything. It's scary to walk round and see everything from Christian clothing, Christian nick-nacks and Christian albums to Jesus dolls, luminous crosses and Ten Commandment tea towels. If it had Jesus' name on it, it was there. There was even a famous actor walking around dressed up in full Superman gear, but with a 'B' on his chest instead of an 'S'. He turned out to be 'Bibleman', and he wandered around the venue for four days solid shouting out random passages from the good book.

We were sat in our own little booth giving away copies of the album, when Sophie whispered in my ear, 'I just wonder if Jesus would come in here and turn the tables over.' I felt the same; that there was something not quite right about much of this multi-billion-dollar machine that calls itself the American Christian industry.

Somewhere along the road it had moved well away from the Carpenter of Nazareth by opting for 'Bibleman' and perfect smiles. It was a distant and unrecognisable relation to the radical movement that is Christianity.

This set the tone for us, and there has always been a tension between this gigantic industry and our own beliefs about God. That doesn't mean that it's been all bad, for we've been out to America a few times and have met some quality people. Certainly there are some Christian bands made up of good lads who want to sing for Jesus, yet time and again they seem to be sucked into this huge Christian machine. It makes me sad to see them spending ten months of the year touring from big Christian gig to big Christian gig, being cooped up on a tour bus with virtually no fellowship outside the band. There are some who, to be honest, have lost the plot, who don't know why they are doing it any more but have to keep on singing about Jesus to sell the units.

America is a strange place. As the biggest Christian country in the world, there is a Christian version of everything you can think of (Christian midwives, Christian mechanics, even Christian dog trainers). It scares me that America produces 90 per cent of the world's Christian resources and yet it is a country where there are frightening levels of violence, crime, immorality, suicide and family breakdown. In so many ways it has missed the point of true Christianity, but still the majority of the population call themselves Christians.

A lot of Christians seem to think that if you tithe to

the church, buy your Christian CDs and books, and call yourself a Christian, then you can relax. They think that once you've got this sussed, then your ticket to heaven is guaranteed and you don't have to worry about all that boring lifestyle stuff. Now all of this might be a bit cheeky coming from a Brit, and I also know there is an awful lot of it going on in the church in Britain, but – and perhaps this is due to size – the problem seems to be more intense in America.

Not that we weren't tempted. While we've never had any trouble walking down the street at home, there were times in America when we would have to run to our limos to avoid getting mobbed by the mass of screaming fans chasing after us. At one festival people were even queuing up for two and a half hours to get our autographs. However, it was never too hard to resist the temptation to take all of this sort of caper seriously; we poked fun at it (we still do) and reminded ourselves of what we're all about. It's amazing how much thinking about the broken lives in Manchester brings you back down to earth when you're standing on a stage in front of 50,000 screaming Christians. What was tempting, though, was the idea that if we took just six months out from schools work we could fund the ministry for years to come. It almost seemed plausible, but when lined up against our three original principles – Manchester, the Bible and the lost – we knew that it wasn't right.

As I said earlier, there was something different about the men in suits from Warner Alliance. They were extremely godly people who understood my concerns. They were also determined to put all their weight behind *We Don't Get What We Deserve*, which they launched with a fanfare in June 1996. They hired a red London double-decker bus and drove around Nashville with assorted industry personnel on board, ending up at the Sherlock Holmes pub for fish and chips. I think they fully expected the Tribe to be the next big thing in America, to sell half a million copies and make them loads of money, and looking back, I think we were half-expecting it as well. We went over to perform at the few gigs we could, all of which seemed to confirm that the kids were well up for it. However, after a while it was clear that for some reason the album wasn't going to be the big success many of us had hoped for. American sales peaked at around 50,000 copies, and I think every-one was a little bit disappointed.

There wasn't much time for feeling miserable, for as soon as we arrived home we got straight back into the schools and started working on a new project. We were still scratching our heads to try and come up with ways of helping to support all the young Christians who were dotted around the Manchester area. We had an idea for a monthly meeting where people could get together for an evening of radical worship with videos, flashing lights, dancers and all the other stuff the Tribe had become known for. As well as some bangingly loud music, we also wanted to provide clear Bible teaching and a chance for the kids to meet other new Christians. As many of these kids were being fed into churches that were struggling to support them, these Planet Life services seemed like a decent idea.

We all know that the big problem facing the church in Britain is the lack of teenagers. Sadly, what few there are seem to be leaving the church faster than ever before, despite all our fine talk about revival. If we could just hold on to our teenagers, we would be back into a period of growth. But that seems easier said than done, and most of the kids who become Christians through the Tribe's schools missions are still going to churches where they are one of only a handful of teenagers. Planet Life was set up to bring together a few hundred of them, fire them up and send them back to their churches to keep going and keep pressing on.

We realised that a traditional worship band format wasn't really going to work for us, so Zarc got on with the job of churning out funky versions of traditional Christian worship songs. We were also trying to write some songs of our own that could be used in the service, and ended up with enough material for a whole album. And so *Jumping in the House of God* came into being, having been recorded at Zarc's studio during August 1996. Warner Alliance got to hear it and liked it, but as they'd spent so much cash promoting *We Don't Get What We Deserve*, and had had little return for their money, the plans for the release of *Jumping* were a little less ambitious.

At the time Warner Alliance sent it out to the Christian bookshops across the country, and it automatically got sent out to every Warner Brothers employee in

America, about 3,000 in all. Usually this wouldn't have been such a big deal, as due to the size of the company the complimentary box of weekly releases that landed on every employee's desk would often contain 30 or 40 CDs. The week that *Jumping* came out it was the only one in the box. Instead of putting it in the bin, most of Warner Brothers that week were listening to *Jumping in the House of God*. Among them was the boss of it all, who went wild over the track called 'The real thing'. He phoned up Chris Hauser, our promotions man at Warner Alliance, and told him first that it was a hit and, secondly, that it was to be put out to the mainstream immediately.

Sure enough, the guys in LA got fired up about the single and started pumping it out to mainstream radio. Several of the major stations across the country started playing it like mad, and it wasn't long before all that initial enthusiasm looked as if it was going to pay off. It went top twenty in many of the singles charts across the country, and many people thought that it was going to sell a million copies. At one stage we had a phone call from one of the big guys from Warner Brothers in LA saying, in between puffs on a fat cigar, 'We are going to make you very rich men!' They even flew a few people out to Manchester especially to tell us this, as if being told it face to face would somehow make it more real.

When the time came for the single to be distributed to the shops and go on sale to the general public something went wrong. The distribution didn't quite happen the way it needed to, and it ended up at number 22 in the billboard dance charts. Not that we weren't happy with this, but it wasn't quite the global domination the suits had predicted. I'm convinced that they weren't trying to hype us up; that they genuinely believed that the single could have been a hit. Certainly our friends at the Christian label Warner Alliance had never known anything like it. There are times when I wonder whether it was God who pulled the plug on the whole thing. Perhaps the worst thing that could have happened to the Tribe at that point would have been having a massive hit and making piles of money. It would have distracted us from the need to build up a core of faithful prayer supporters who give us a few quid a month and help us do what we do.

I got this idea from Billy Graham's autobiography. There's a passage near the beginning where he was spending a lot of time fund-raising, visiting hundreds of churches in attempts to raise support. A millionaire (rumour has it that it was John Paul Getty) volunteered totally to underwrite his ministry, offering to pour in millions of dollars over the years. Billy would be freed up from time-consuming fund-raising, allowing him to concentrate solely on preaching the gospel. Billy, to his eternal credit, told the wealthy man that he couldn't take his money. Instead of solving all his problems with a simple 'yes', Billy knew that he had to rely on those people who give five or ten dollars each month. Yes, the money was the same, but those small and regular donations came with something else: prayer support and ownership of the vision.

In many ways I wasn't spiritual enough to turn my back on 'The real thing' in the way that Billy Graham turned his back on his own cash incentive. There was never any question that we would have used all the money to spread the gospel, but it could have distracted us from building that prayer support. It is so important that a ministry is based on a firm foundation of the prayers of faithful people. If our prayer supporters found out that we were making millions of pounds from selling records all over the world, who could blame them for giving their £5, £10 or £20 a month to other ministries that needed it more than we did?

So the chance of having a major hit came and went. In hindsight I'm glad it did. I don't think the Tribe will ever become a million-selling outfit. Instead of making a fortune, I think we will sell just enough. These days less than 10 per cent of our income as a ministry comes from the Tribe, and the rest comes from those faithful, committed prayer supporters who give to us every month. That is our financial DNA, and we need to remember that as the ministry grows, the core of our support is those people who give faithfully.

As the word continued to spread around the world we started to get bigger gig offers, which became increasingly difficult to turn down. One year we were invited to the DOVE awards (the American Christian music awards in Nashville) and Warner Alliance were trying to set things up so that we could present one of the awards. As over 70 million people watch it on TV, it's kind of a big deal, and so it was with great delight that I told the men in suits that the Tribe couldn't present an award as we would be working in Ramsbottom High School for the week. Maybe there was a kind of inverted snobbery at work, but we loved turning down these massive gigs all over the world. Compared to getting stuck into a secondary school, gigs in football stadiums and TV appearances were no competition.

We can't have offended too many people, however, as the next year (1998) we were invited back. As we weren't in school at the time, Elaine Hanley (one of our singers) and I popped over for a few days. Instead of presenting an award this time around, we were faced with the even more frightening prospect of being nominated for a couple of awards ourselves. As if that wasn't enough, two film crews came along with us – one from the BBC filming an *Everyman* documentary and one from a programme that was on Channel 4 at the time called *Alpha Zone*.

As we waited during the ceremony it was strange to think that no British band had ever won a DOVE before, and that if we didn't win, it was going to be totally embarrassing with the TV crews there. Thankfully, we won them both: Best Dance Album and Best Dance Single. After the ceremony Elaine and I went backstage for a press conference with the waiting media. Receiving the awards had been one of the most nerve-wracking occasions in my life, and my adrenaline was pumping. I was trying to work out what to say to the media, and from what I had heard, the standard thing was to say lots of 'thank yous'. That seemed like a bit of a waste and I thought it would be better if I just said what was on my heart. So I did a little preach. I told them that I had met some great people since I had been in America, but I had also met a lot of people who had lost the plot. There were loads who had been called to be evangelists just like the World Wide Message Tribe but who had got sucked into the whole Christian music scene. I told them how good I thought it would be if they would discover a passion for the lost and get fired up to get out there instead of being happily sucked into this bubble of money, fame and adulation.

I think people were quite surprised. A few minutes later I was queuing up to go into more media things and Elaine and I were holding our two DOVE awards each, when Toby from DC Talk came up behind us. He's a good lad, but Americans aren't great at getting the irony in our sense of humour. DC Talk usually win an armful of these awards, but this year they hadn't released any material and had only picked up one, so as Toby walked up behind us I turned round and started singing, à la Old Trafford, Stretford end, '2:1, 2:1, 2:1!' Toby looked worried, and quietly asked me if I was all right and still managing not to let things go to my head. My heart sank as he really hadn't got the joke. I couldn't bring myself to explain, so I just went red and kept my mouth shut.

Anyone who knows anything about pop music, particularly the type of music that the Tribe are into, will know that it's a young man's game. In 1995, not long after things really started to take off, I was almost 35. I've never seen myself as a rapper or musician, and I started to become increasingly aware of the need for somebody to come into the band and take my place. I had taken on the role of fronting the band and doing the preaching but, as the ministry was growing and we were taking on more people, there were so many demands on my time to try and keep things on track. Mark, Zarc and I met, and decided to pray that God would give us a killer front man – not just somebody who could rap, sing and dance, but somebody who could preach as well. I firmly believe that God went out and saved the best possible person for that job. His name is Cameron Dante.

5

The Real Thing

As you can imagine, Cameron Dante didn't start life with such a glamorous name. He was born in Salford, one of Manchester's toughest areas, and by the time he got to secondary school he was well into sniffing glue and lighter fluid, spending large parts of his day getting high and hanging out with his Salford scally mates. Sometimes they got a bit creative, practising their home-tattooing techniques on each other. Cameron's chest and arms bear a couple of choice tattoos (his old name is written in three-inch-high letters across his chest, and MAGIC MUSHROOMS appears down his arm).

He got into breakdancing at the age of 13 and started a troop with Howard and Jason, who later went on to become two of the quieter members of Take That. They practised for up to four hours each day, six days a week. Eventually they became UK breakdancing champions and came third in the world championships. At the same time as these successes throughout his school years, Cameron was working his way through the drugs on offer in the city. As so often happens, he went from sniffing glue and lighter fluid to amphetamines, cocaine and even on to heroin.

When he was 17 he headed off to Benidorm with £80 in his pocket. By the time he got to Calais he'd spent most of his cash, leaving himself with £20 to get across Europe. Being a bit of a resourceful young man, Cam made his way down the Continent by a combination of petty thieving and hitch-hiking. Once he had arrived at Benidorm he headed for the clubs to do what he did best and make his living breakdancing.

Having been at it for about three months, things changed when the club's DJ was sacked. Cam was offered the slot and despite the fact that he had never done it before, it didn't take him long to master the decks and work out how to hype up the crowd. He was in his element; the club absolutely rocked and over the next three years he grew to become a pretty well-known DJ in Benidorm, Ibiza and Madrid, making a nice living for himself.

The success wasn't always such a good thing, though. One day the rival club from the other side of the street decided that they wanted Cam for themselves. They offered it to him nicely (more money, more drugs) and when he refused, they sent a couple of bouncers over, who tied him to a chair and threw him into a swimming pool. All he remembers is thinking that he was going to die and crying out for his mum.

As he got more and more into the club scene Cameron took more and more drugs, resulting in a fairly hazy three-year period. It all came to an end when he was walking down a street in Benidorm and a woman he'd known for years in Salford – the mother of a mate of his – walked past him. He ran up to her saying, 'Look, it's me – Cameron,' but she didn't even recognise him. He knew the lifestyle was beginning to catch up with him, so he decided that it was time to come back to Manchester. He came back via Birmingham, where he made a living selling drugs and DJ-ing before he landed a job as a resident DJ in one of the biggest nightclubs in Manchester.

Out in Madrid he'd met some guys who were forming a band called Bizarre Inc, and once he was back in Britain he got in touch and started going out with one of the dancers. Having heard him rap, the band asked if he fancied joining them on their forthcoming tour. Their first single ('Playing with knives') was starting to be a hit in the clubs, and when it was followed up with another track called 'I'm gonna get you', the band was launched big time. It got to number three in the charts and was followed up with several more hits in Britain. Then 'I'm gonna get you' hit it in the States, and for a year the band really did have it made. They travelled everywhere first class and had as many limos, as much money and as many drugs and girls as they wanted. Cam lived the wild pop-star lifestyle, but at the end of the year they brought out a single called 'Took my love'. It made the top 20, but was nowhere near as big a success as the previous single. The record company got a bit nervous and the all-important buzz seemed to desert the band.

Cam returned to England and decided to try and do some of his own stuff. Zarc knew Cameron's manager, and he was booked into Zarc's Perfect Music studio in Cheadle Hulme. Zarc happens to be one of the mildest people I know; at the time Cam was a wild, drugged-out, profane wreck. The project he was working on was for an act called Vertigo, which was made up of Cam, another bloke and Cleo Roccus (a 1980s TV personality famous for her extensive cleavage). One of the tracks that had been chosen to launch this pop phenomenon was called 'Beneath the sheets'. Despite this, Zarc could see something special in this lovable rogue. It was obvious that he was a brilliant rapper and dancer, but Zarc also thought he might make a good communicator. He told Mark and me, and the three of us committed ourselves to praying for him every day. We had started to talk to him about our faith, and felt for sure that a verse in 2 Corinthians 4 was appropriate. 'The god of this age has blinded the minds of unbelievers' seemed to describe what had happened to Cam. I really believe that there is a veil over the eyes of every person who isn't a Christian. That applies not only to people who are wild drug addicts like Cameron was, but also to nice sweet people who don't know Jesus. Prayer is the key to lifting the veil, even though it can take a long time.

We prayed hard for this to happen to Cameron, and gradually we were sure that our prayers were being answered. First of all he started showing more of an interest in Christian things. Zarc had told him that he was a Christian, but he hadn't really spent a lot of time talking to him about his faith. Cam, however, started asking loads of questions. Then he bought a book on comparative religions. To add to our excitement, he then bought Zarc a bottle of champagne with a little tag on it saying 'Thanks for all your spiritual encouragement'. I told him that we'd crack that bottle the day he became a Christian. He looked at me as if to say 'fat chance', but the more we prayed the closer he came. Once he, Zarc and I went out for a drink and I started asking him about where he was at with God. It was obvious God was at work in his life and that it wasn't going to be long before he became a Christian.

Our Planet Life services were starting to take off, with hundreds of young people turning up to the monthly services. Zarc invited Cam along to one of them. He hadn't been to church since he was a young Catholic lad in Salford, except to Zarc's wedding. While the wedding service itself didn't have him repenting on his knees, he did comment to us on the way out, 'They've upped it a bit since I was a lad.' It was to his surprise and ours that he accepted one of Zarc's invites to a Planet Life service some time later. Once he had plucked up the courage to come in he found a big lighting rig, PA, video screens and all the other stuff that made sense to him.

We had a Canadian evangelist called Mike Hack speaking that night, and what he said all seemed to make sense to Cameron. When he had finished he invited anybody who wanted to become a Christian to stand up. This wasn't really the done thing at Planet Life, and in fact I had told Mike not to do it because it seemed like such a typical thing to do. For a long time the only person in the church who stood up was Cameron. He says it felt as if he could hear the wind whistling through the church. To this day he doesn't know why he stood up. He says it was as if the Lord dragged him to his feet, but he really did want to give his life to Jesus. He went down the front after that service and talked to Mike, who suggested they both meet up the next day. He could see that Cameron was a guy who needed a lot of help, so he agreed to go and meet him in his nightclub the next day.

Mike Hack is an international evangelist, and he just happened to have six days left in Britain before he had to return home. He spent most of them with Cam, putting him into a spiritual incubator. Mike went down to his nightclub and read the Bible to him while he DJ-ed, surrounded by half-naked women dancing on the podiums. He went to his house and taught him the Bible, took him to church, introduced him to loads of Christians and took him round for meals at various Christian homes. He just fed him and gave him in six days the most intensive discipleship programme. It was exactly what Cameron needed.

The night Cameron gave his life to Christ I remember going back to Zarc's house and having a little party. We got the bottle of champagne, shook it up and said, 'This is the night we have been waiting and praying for . . . You're in!' I was so glad that Mike Hack took him on and gave him the time that was needed. So often we fail to invest in baby Christians, especially ones like Cameron who desperately need the support.

Zarc and Mark were at this point working on our latest new track, 'The real thing'. Cameron was so fired up and excited that he rushed off and wrote a rap about being a Christian, and recorded it double quick with Zarc for his new track. He also told his girlfriend, Vicky, but she didn't quite share his sense of excitement. He had met Vicky in a gay nightclub in Manchester – they were the only two straight people in the place – and they had fallen in love and been living together for a couple of years. The trouble was that Vicky had had all sorts of problems in the past – she had suffered terrible sexual abuse as a child and felt that God had let her down – and the last thing she wanted was a religious boyfriend. When Cam rushed into their house and told her his news she walked out and went back home to Scotland for two weeks. But in a way, even that was God's timing, as Cameron was left in the hands of Mike Hack, and then myself and others could invest time in this baby Christian.

Vicky returned and had decided that she really did love Cam, even if he was a Christian and had gone a bit weird. I wasn't too thrilled with the idea of them continuing to live together because I knew they would climb into the same double bed that they had been sleeping in over the past two years, but I didn't know how to challenge Cam about it. We were teaching him things from the Bible and I felt at that time that God spoke to me and told me not to come down too heavily on him and Vicky. Instead it seemed to make sense to teach him the word and let the Holy Spirit do the rest.

We were praying that God would speak to Cam about this relationship with Vicky and in an amazing roundabout way He did. Vicky was thinking of ways to get Cam off his religious trip, so one night, lying in bed, she told him that if he really was a Christian he wouldn't be sleeping with her. She thought that, when it came down to a choice between God and sex, Cam would choose sex every time. Instead he simply agreed and got out of bed, went downstairs and slept on the settee. He slept there for the next nine months until they got married.

We kept on praying, and tried to encourage Cam as much as we could, but we also started doubling our prayers for Vicky. Cam was desperate for her to become a Christian, but it seemed an almost impossible prospect; if most people have a veil over their eyes, Vicky had a double-thick duvet over hers. In many ways she hated us Christians who were involved in changing her boyfriend into a Jesus freak. One of the problems for her was that Cameron was actually a nicer bloke to have around now that he was a Christian. He was a more considerate, kinder boyfriend, and of course he had been completely delivered and healed of his drug addiction. Much as it offended her, she also had loads of people praying like mad for her. Bit by bit the double-thick duvet was lifting and, as Cameron lived the life and prayed the prayers, Vicky got more and more interested.

After about three months she agreed to go along to a 'discovering Christianity' course at the local church. They let her ask all her questions and present all her problems, and on the last day she had a real encounter with God, sensing Him for the first time. We were so thrilled and were convinced that this was the moment we had all been waiting for.

The next night she went to hear me preach at a Planet Life service in Cheadle. I spoke about being hot or cold, about being on fire for God or sacking Christianity, explaining how it wasn't enough just to be in the middle. Rather than deciding that, yes, she was going to be hot, Vicky doubted whether she really did have it in her to be sold out for God. Instead she decided that she was better off being cold. It wasn't quite the reaction I had hoped for when I prepared the message, and immediately she went back into her old lifestyle, full of clubs and drugs.

It was another five months before we could get Vicky to go to anything else remotely Christian. Cameron was pleading with her to come with us all to Spring Harvest, as by this stage he had joined the Tribe (rapping, singing and doing a little bit of speaking). Eventually she gave in, but agreed to go for only one night. It was the big Easter weekend in Manchester and the clubs were open all night. She spent the weekend off her face on drugs, but everywhere she went she seemed to be confronted by God. She met Christians whenever she left the house, and when she was at home people kept on phoning her up, talking to her about the Lord. She couldn't get away from God, and she was feeling pretty stubborn about things when she went to Spring Harvest. They both went into a meeting where Roger Mitchell was speaking. Towards the end of the meeting, during which Cam had been praying like mad, Roger said exactly the same thing as Mike Hack had said eight months before. To Cam's amazement, Vicky stood up and gave her life to the Lord.

We were preparing for a concert in another venue at Spring Harvest. Vicky had always been very cold towards me, but as she walked into the room and gave me a massive hug, I looked at her face and could see a clear, physical transformation. The hardness had gone, replaced by a softness in her face and a joy that could mean only one thing. I jumped up onto the dressing-table and shouted, 'I can't believe it! Vicky's become a Christian!' The dressing-table snapped off the wall and collapsed with a great crack. Later I had to crawl to the stage manager in the hope that he wouldn't get too mad.

In so many ways Vicky has become the perfect partner for Cam. Because of all that she has been through she has a tender heart, and after having a shell of hardness and being so opposed to God, she has softened up so much. A few weeks later Cam and Vicky were baptised together in the same baptismal pool during an incredible service. A week later they got married and changed their names by deed poll to Cameron and Tori Dante. Finally Cam was able to go back upstairs to his double bed – this time with his wife.

Cam's arrival was a double bonus for me. Not only did he bring to the band his wicked talents as a dancer and rapper, but he so obviously had the heart and the gift of an evangelist right from the very start. It didn't take long to notice that when he spoke, young people wanted to listen. I committed myself to try and invest time in Cam, to teach him the Bible and help him grow. I really believed that he was the guy to fill my shoes in the Tribe; not just to front the band but also to preach.

In May 1998 I did my last concert with the Tribe, and a week later I went to the first schools mission that the Tribe were performing without me either as an evangelist or a member of the band. It was a very weird thing to watch the kids jumping up and down just as much as they usually did. Cameron came up to preach the gospel, and he preached well. When he did his appeal and invited the young people to go into classrooms, it was the biggest response we had ever seen at a schools concert. I sat at the side of this room as the kids poured in – 106 of them – thinking that it was as if God were saying, 'Do you really think it was ever about you?'

Since then Cameron has developed a heart and passion to become an evangelist. The most exciting thing I've ever witnessed in my life is not just the conversion of this couple – these two people who were about as far away from God as possible – but the thousands of young people who have been affected by them. The lesson screams itself out loud from their lives: no heart is too hard to be broken into by the love of God.

6

People

By the spring of 1997, with Cameron growing like mad as both a Christian and a communicator, it became clear that it would soon be time for me to hang up my rapping boots and get on with heading up the fast-expanding ministry. We also decided that we should try to stop shuffling the line-up and get six people whom we could record the next album with and who could stick together at least until summer 2000.

Cameron's arrival had a significant impact on the band and the way things worked, but over the years there have been plenty of other developments within the line-up. In fact, the decision to use the word 'tribe' in the name has turned out to be kind of appropriate. Instead of being a set group of people who make up the band from beginning to end, the Tribe is more of a collective.

When things started out there were four of us in the

band: myself, Mark, Elaine Hanley and Lorraine Williams, plus, of course, non-performing member Zarc. The numbers soon grew as we took on more dancers, including Zarc's wife Miriam, Collette Nuttall (who, with her husband Dave, was the first person to move into the Wythenshawe Eden project), Vicky Holt, Sophie Woodward and Lorretta Andrews. In fact, the Tribe has had quite a high turnover of dancers, pushing the total up to almost twenty in five years. As you can imagine, they get worked pretty hard.

It wasn't long before we felt the need to get another wailing woman on board to help out with the singing. Eventually we came across Sani, a fantastic woman from Swaziland. Back home she had seen the country go through an incredible revival, one that was jam-packed with the most extraordinary miracles. She arrived in Manchester with all kinds of stories of a powerful move of God, especially in her own life. When she was younger, Sani's father was the king's private secretary, and he actually led the king of Swaziland to the Lord. She told us about a tradition within the land that each year the king takes a new wife for himself, who joins the others in his vast harem. The king's son set about carrying on the custom for himself once he was on the throne. He saw Sani and invited her to be his Mrs 1989, but somehow she managed to defy all the odds and get out of it. She ended up in Britain and became a member of the World Wide Message Tribe. She was an awesome singer and an amazing schools worker, yet after about 18 months her visa ran out and she had to

go back to Swaziland. Her departure left us with something of a hole.

God seems to have a knack of filling holes. Not long
after Sani was back in Swaziland we met the lovely Beth
Vickers. She wailed her way through a couple of years
with the Tribe, after which she felt called by God to go
and work for Soul Survivor. She moved down south, fell
in love with their worship leader and became Mrs Matt
Redman.

Shortly after Beth left, it was time for Elaine Hanley
and me to do our last gig as well. Mark had stopped
performing a year before, choosing instead to take
charge of the choreography and the show, plus starting
an exciting new ministry called Kik-Start (later renamed
Innervation) with a vision to reproduce some of the stuff
that we had seen in Manchester around the country.
Elaine and I were the last of the original line-up to go.
For me, there was so much else to do for Message to
Schools, and for Elaine, it was time to get on with looking after her new baby, Nadine (although I know that as
long as God gives her breath she'll always be singing for
Him). The farewell gig took place in front of 7,000
screaming teenagers on 8 May 1998, and I was
presented with a golden boot in recognition of my
talents as a foot stamper.

What the Tribe was left with was something special: a
team of six who managed to keep true to the original
spirit of the band at the same time as moving it on in
time with the rest of the culture. Together, Cameron,
Deronda, Tim, Emma, Colette and Claire were the Tribe

mark 3. Each of them brought something fresh to the band, and each had a story to tell.

Like Cameron, Deronda Lewis's testimony is pretty extraordinary. Brought up in Tulsa, Oklahoma, her mother was only 14 when she found out she was pregnant, and before Deronda's first birthday, her mother had given birth to a second child, Deronda's little sister. Their dad was an alcoholic, and he was often violent. It was not a happy home to grow up in, and by the time she was six, Deronda was taken away from her parents and was living with her grandmother – a deeply religious woman who went to church six nights a week. Every night after church, Deronda would hear her grandmother crying out in prayer, 'Dear Jesus, please save my babies. Don't let them go to hell.' But all this seemed to do was turn her off God, and she chose instead to have a go at enjoying herself with her friends.

When she was 16 her grandmother gave her a choice: either she could carry on living with her, or she could go back to what was left of her parents' home. They were two extremes, with the strict rules of her grandmother at one end, and the complete freedom of her mother at the other. Deronda went for what she thought was the best option, and moved back to be with her mum, settling down into a life of constant partying and entertainment. Her life was suddenly different, and of course she thought she was really living.

Deronda started dating a boy from one of the area's big drug-pushing families, getting sucked into the accompanying lifestyle. She remembers watching in horror when her boyfriend's brother was killed next to her in a drive-by shooting. All kinds of crazy things were going on, and by the time she was 17 she was pregnant. At 18 she was arrested and put in jail for stealing from a store where she'd worked. The store management were keen to throw the book at her and her lawyer warned her that she could be looking at as many as ten years in jail. Deronda lay terrified in the prison cell as all the other women were taunting and teasing her. She refused to cry, but begged God to get her out of there and save her from jail. At the trial the next day the judge let her go with a warning that if he ever saw her again she would be spending a very long time behind bars. She returned to her boyfriend and for six months struggled to live as a Christian.

It wasn't until she moved to New York to try and make a break that God really got hold of her. She pulled into a petrol station just outside the city and the attendant asked her if she was new in town, suggesting that she go along with him to church. This meeting seemed to set the tone for Deronda, and for the next few days it was as if everywhere she went she encountered only Christians. She went to church and found it wasn't the sombre religious thing she experienced at home, but that the place was full of funky, vibrant people who were sold out to Jesus. With the help of the church she finally started to grow as a Christian, and has spent the last 20 years singing with some of the gospel greats in America, from Al Green to Carlton Pearson.

We came across her in one of those funny, round-about, God ways. We were looking for a singer after Beth had decided she was going to move on to Soul Survivor, and we met a band called Raze. Both Raze and the Tribe were performing at a festival in America, and I was completely blown away by Donni, their awesome singer. Perhaps it was slightly naughty of me, but I mentioned to Donni that if ever things didn't work out with her and Raze she should get in touch.

'Well,' said Donni, 'I'm happy with Raze, but my mum could be interested.'

'Your mum?' I thought she was joking, and was just about to explain the difference between us and Johnny Mathis when she started telling us what a great gospel singer her mother was.

We prayed about it, phoned Deronda and brought her over to Manchester, having only heard one of her demo tapes. She turned out to be the most scarily godly, laid-back grandmother you could ever meet. She looked about 25 but was actually 40 years old and full of the Holy Spirit. We all agreed that she was the one for the job, and if ever we needed proof, it came when we saw how powerfully her singing and testimony moved people in schools.

They might not have come quite as far as Deronda, but Tim and Emma Owen have also been vital to the development of the Tribe into what it is today. Tim was with the band RE:Fresh for a couple of years in Bristol and Emma was a police officer when they fell in love in London. She had a nasty accident and was pensioned off from the police with a bad back. In true God-like style, Emma got healed sufficiently so that she could strut her stuff for the Tribe. Tim and Emma auditioned for the band, and we were all totally excited about them. Emma particularly is a magnet for young people and we often used to see lots of little girls at concerts dressed up exactly like her with their baggy pants, plaits and goggles. Emma's the one who gets more letters than anybody in the office, asking all kinds of questions. She is the kind of girl who has been through all sorts of stuff as a teenager; rebelling and turning away from God, as well as struggling with an eating disorder. There are so many people we meet who can relate to what she's been through, and from her position now of being well on fire for Jesus, Emma is able to help loads of people. Recently God has given her and the inimitable Dawn Reynolds a vision for a new ministry called Girl International, which aims to help and empower young women to be all they can be in God.

Colette Smethurst joined shortly before Tim and Emma, getting on board as a dancer and schools worker. Colette was actually the unofficial leader of the Tribe. She organised the schools missions and kept things together, doing far more than she originally signed up for. This was all due to the fact that Colette is the original hide-your-light-under-a-bushel person. It was ages before we realised that she had a fantastic voice and she ended up singing on our albums and leading worship at Planet Life. She also showed plenty of skill as an administrator, and is just an all-round sickeningly talented woman. Yet despite all this she didn't always enjoy performing with the World Wide Message Tribe. She often had to drag herself onto stage to leap around and grin at all the masses at the concerts. Her heart was really into small group discipleship, and she was one of the first people to live in the inner city with Eden. Within a few months of moving in there she fell in love with the team leader, Mark Smethurst, and they got married.

Colette, like Emma, also struggled with an eating disorder when she was younger. For years they both suffered with their self-esteem and it amazes me that two women who are so obviously beautiful and talented could believe the devil when he told them they were naff.

I was at one Planet Life service when Emma and Colette were dancing and the aforementioned Dawn Reynolds (who is another all-round gorgeous and gifted girl) was speaking. She mentioned that, as a teenager, she had felt really bad about herself and had become bulimic. I thought to myself that the devil is such a bore, lying to all these girls, telling them they are useless in the pathetic hope they will believe him and waste their lives.

Girls all over the place need to learn not to believe the lies of the one the Bible calls the deceiver and the accuser of the brothers (and sisters!). Instead they need to believe that Jesus made each of them unique with something wonderful to show the world about God. He also thought they were so fantastic that He went all the way and gave His life for them.

Finally, in the Tribe mark 3, there was curly Claire Prosser who for several years was actually the woman in the office who sorted me out, running my diary, typing my letters and generally making sense of all my disorganisation. Claire didn't have a terrible background; she grew up in a nice part of Crawley with Beth Redman and landed herself a good job at the bank. Things were all going well for her when God called her into Manchester, auditioning for the band as a dancer.

With these six making the line-up for the band nice and solid, we got down to the business of recording our next album, *Heatseeker*. Of all the projects we had ever undertaken, *Heatseeker* involved the biggest struggle. This wasn't caused by a lack of ideas; it was actually a result of having too many of them. Cameron was mad about the trashing hard-core dance of Chemical Brothers and the Prodigy. Deronda is the ultimate soul diva and Tim and Emma were more on the pop tip. All I could think of saying was, 'Can't we have more of those funny noises?' It was hard work and nearly led to our producer Zarc having a nervous breakdown. The final result, we think, does have some good moments, but it sounds more like a dance compilation CD than a band with a clear direction in mind. It was to our great surprise therefore when in spring 1999 it won another DOVE award for us. This time no one was able to go and collect it as the heads were well and truly buried in a school in Bury.

Next up came *Frantik*, released in the autumn of

1999, with a much more homogenous sound and a much less stressful recording process. I remember that at the time, however, we did feel the pressure was on a bit. Not only did it need to be good for the Manchester schoolies but also for all sorts of discipleship resources that were spinning off it for the huge bash in the summer of 2000 – but more on that later.

Unlike other bands, we're not out to make music that we necessarily think is cool. We're not even out to make music that we think will sell. We like to think our eyes are blinkered and pointing solely in the direction of 14-year-old Manchester school kids; if they like it then we're happy. The only way we consider an album to have been a success is if it goes down a bomb on a Friday schools gig in Salford.

One of the amazing things about the last few years has been that whenever we have needed somebody, God has provided. God has provided money as well as people, but if I'm honest, it's the people that really amaze me. Giving money is easy for God to do – He is, after all, the Creator and Owner of the entire universe. When it comes to people, however, things get a bit more complicated. Our free will and consciousness can often get in the way of God's plans, but time and again we have been blessed with some absolutely top workers. We've worked alongside so many people with a heart for schools work; people who want to do the hard graft, to bust their gut going into schools day after day. There have been people who have come into Manchester and caught this vision for revival.

As it is a lot harder for God to find people who are prepared to lay down their lives than people who can give a few quid, I take great heart from the way the team has grown. As well as the members of the band, there are now about 60 other people working full time and hundreds more who volunteer. What amazes me is that we regularly get cheques in at the office from the volunteers, the guys who spend most of their spare time stewarding our concerts, selling our merchandise, rigging PA systems or loading vans late into the night. I find it hard to understand how they give so much time without getting paid and still they want to give us money. I know that God will bless them. They are the real heroes of the Message and what's going on in Manchester, not the names of the band. But these secret people who counsel kids week after week, who pray like mad for us week after week, who send us £5 and £10 postal orders every week, and the Eden volunteers who live alongside young people in tough estates – they are the glue that holds it all together.

I get the impression that God views things slightly differently from the way we do. We may think that it is fantastic for us to stand before thousands of screaming kids, but what really counts is time on our knees on our own before God. Add to that a desire to give sacrificially, as well as holiness and all the other stuff that really hurts, and you start to get a fuller picture of what Christianity is all about. They are the things that I think we will receive an eternal reward for, and the people who are on stage must never forget that.

Occasionally I get a little worried that maybe we've received a lot of our reward in advance through all the praise we get. It often feels weird that people can say, 'Andy Hawthorne [or the Tribe] led me to Jesus,' when all we have done is performed at a gig or preached a sermon. The real reward will go to those faithful secret ones who have prayed, served and ministered behind the scenes so these people could come to know Jesus.

7

Discovering Eden

There have probably only been three occasions in my life when I have been sure that God has spoken to me big style. On each of these, it has been so obviously Him that I have had no other option than to get on with what He has told me to do. This first happened when I was a teenager, and I sat in a church listening to my brother's testimony, suddenly convinced that I had to do all I could to get back to God. The second time was when we started the Message. I was in bed reading through the book of Isaiah, and as I made my way through chapter 43, the 'rivers in the desert' and the 'streams in the wasteland' seemed to have been written especially for the work we were about to start. The most recent occasion was the time when we had come up with the idea for a project called 'Eden'.

The Tribe had been getting on with schools work for about four years, during which time we had always tried to concentrate on the rougher areas. Somehow it made sense to be wanting to target the places that had the least, but our work was taking us in (literally) the opposite direction. Instead of the inner-city estates we were spending much of our time in the suburbs. In these wealthy areas the churches had many more resources and were a lot better equipped to hang on to the new Christians that appeared after our week-long missions. This was the problem: when we did missions in the inner city, just as many young people responded and they seemed to be just as up for God despite all their problems, yet there was very little for them to get stuck into. Without the Christians living around them it was no wonder they struggled to keep going.

The church has simply not been cutting it with those people. We have failed to understand quite what it is like to live on such an estate. We have quaint ideas about these people we label 'working class', yet as many as 75 per cent of the residents are totally reliant on the state. The church has more or less stayed away for the last few generations, leaving the problems to fester and sending a message to the people that it does not care for them at all.

But this doesn't seem to be God's way. Whenever there has been a mighty move of God, it has always been the inner cities that have come to life as the poor get a healthy dose of the good news. This happened alongside the work of great men like William Booth, John Wesley, George Whitefield and Charles Spurgeon. Whether it was Welsh miners or people from the city slums, it was the poor who got the biggest portion.

This has always made sense to us, and so when it became clear that we were spending most of our time in the suburbs, we weren't too comfortable with the idea. I booked up a couple of schools missions in early 1996 in Wythenshawe, one of the biggest council estates in Europe. The schools were keen, but as we looked around for local churches to support the missions we had a bit more trouble. We ended up working with a little church called King's Church which, when we first met, had a congregation totalling 14 adults and six children. The pastor of the church at that time, a man named Adrian Nottingham, had been living in Wythenshawe for 11 years, and virtually every day he walked around the streets calling (quietly) out to God to do something about the terrible state the place was in. We're not just talking about poor street lighting and broken windows here, but a huge pick'n'mix of the worst social problems associated with inner-city life. Things were so rough that Adrian even felt too scared to prayer-walk around the area known as Benchill. This was the most notorious part of the estate and according to official statistics was the number one most-deprived ward in the whole of the UK, the bit known for drive-by shootings, prostitution and chronic drug abuse. Adrian ended up prayer-driving around Benchill, and when I saw it for the first time myself, I knew exactly why he didn't want to get out of the car.

The two schools missions we had booked up on the estate were put on back to back, with a joint concert at the end held in the local forum centre. Both had gone really well, but the run-up to the concert was pretty chaotic. Elaine was ill and couldn't make it, Beth was desperately trying to learn her parts just minutes before the concert began and Cameron was rushing off straight away afterwards to go skiing with Tori. Somehow we didn't have all the equipment we needed, yet 700 teenagers turned up, and after I preached about 100 of them responded.

What was even more awesome was that they all turned up for church on the following Sunday. King's Church put on a special evening service and the congregation rose from about 20 to 120 overnight. Suddenly the church was full of these Wythenshawe scallies, many of whom were really up for God. It was so exciting, and seemed like the direct fulfilling of God's promise about 'rivers in the desert'. Sadly, over the next few months we heard that most of those young people had drifted away from God. To this day there are probably only six of them left in the church. While we're all pleased that their lives have been radically changed, it is impossible not to feel sad for the other 94.

The girls in the Tribe were particularly moved by these two weeks in schools. In their spare time they returned as often as they could, meeting the kids in their homes in an attempt to help the church disciple them. We found that something had happened to each of us, and we couldn't shake the area from our minds. We had clearly seen how much these areas really needed God, and also just how capable He was of changing their lives. It was obvious why many of the baby faiths never made it through the first couple of months, and no one would expect each member of King's Church (children included) to be able to pastor five of these young people who came into the kingdom with tons of problems and needed so much help and support.

I met with my friend Frank Green and talked with him about what we could do about it all. We came up with a mad idea of giving their church the dream ticket for youth work. If we were a small church, we wondered, what would we need to be able to cope with a hundred new Christians? As well as piles of resources and prayer support, we guessed we would probably need 30 or 40 devoted youth workers – not just any youth workers but people who were really fired up about it. In the past there have been plenty of people who have moved onto these tough estates in ones and twos, only to retreat back to suburbia as soon as it all got a bit too hard. It was our thought that we needed so many key youth workers not only to follow up all the young people who would come to faith, but also to provide a network of support and encouragement that comes from being part of a larger community of sold out believers.

Jesus talked about people like these Eden workers as 'the salt of the earth'. In Jesus' day, salt wasn't used for sprinkling on your dinner for a bit of flavour, but in two other key ways: fertilising and disinfecting. Large industrial quantities were shovelled on the soil to make good things grow or (in the case of the primitive toilets they had) to kill off bad things. And that's exactly what happens when large quantities of Christians move into an area like Benchill, choosing to live like the salt of the earth. Good things grow and bad things die off. Is it any wonder that crime comes down?

We also knew we would need a full-time team of three or four to go around the schools and streets in the area, as well as having the Tribe as evangelists whenever necessary. It all sounded like the workings of a deranged mind, but we visited Adrian and offered it to him anyway.

A couple of weeks later, after Adrian had said that he was into the idea, we went to see the church leaders in Manchester. It was the same group that Simon and I had been to see ten years before when we had told them about Message '88. This time around, Simon and I told them how we thought that God might be calling us to set up something new in Wythenshawe, which we wanted to call Eden. We asked them to give their best people to work as missionaries in the area, while we did all we could to make things happen. To our delight, they didn't just say that they would; they were madly enthusiastic about it all, and prayed for us till we left the meeting really fired up.

As Simon and I sat in the car park in Manchester talking about the meeting, a complete stranger came over and knocked on the car window. He said that he didn't know if we were Christians but as he'd been sitting there eating his butties and reading his Bible, he strongly felt that he should come over and read some verses to us. So Simon (being more spiritual than I, who thought the man was obviously a nutter) told him to get in. The guy climbed into the back of the car and said, 'I don't know if you understand this sort of thing, but I really believe that God just spoke to me. He told me to read these verses to you.' With that he started reading Psalm 37:5–11. We sat there with our chins hitting the floor, listening as he read the words:

> Commit your way to the Lord; trust in him and he will do this: He will make your righteousness shine like the dawn, the justice of your cause like the noonday sun. Be still before the Lord and wait patiently for him; do not fret when people succeed in their ways, when they carry out their wicked schemes. Refrain from anger and turn from wrath; do not fret – it leads only to evil. For those who are evil will be cut off, but those who hope in the Lord will inherit the land. A little while, and the wicked will be no more; though you look for them, they will not be found. But the meek will inherit the land and enjoy great peace.

I have since found out that the guy who gave us those words is an awesome man of God who spends about four hours a day praying and hanging out with the Almighty. It was as if God were saying, 'Yes, this is my idea. I have got a heart for the poor and the lost and I am passionate about change in the inner cities. I want to see the strongholds of the enemy broken.' The verses also mention opposition, people succeeding in their wicked ways and people carrying out schemes against each other. We sat in the car after our guest had left us and wondered where this might come from. It was Simon who was right when he suggested that even though we might see wonderful things happen in the toughest areas, we would come up against even tougher opposition in the church.

King's Church, which was a little independent church, was about to become part of Covenant Ministries, which started out of the house church movement. They had been looking for a church to partner them as they reached out to Wythenshawe, and Covenant Ministries seemed like the ideal choice. Eden had not even started at this point, but I had no idea that these links would cause such problems. It turned out that a couple of the churches that were our key supporters heard that we had got involved with a house church (which was kind of true) and some members started spreading rumours about activities that the church was supposed to be involved in (which were definitely untrue). A whispering campaign started that Andy, Mark and the Tribe had got involved with a dodgy movement and were trying to force people out of the mainstream conservative evangelical churches and into their work in Wythenshawe.

It was just unbelievable; not only were the rumours false, but they started to have an effect on other supporters as well. All sorts of people were pulling their support and some were doing more than their fair share to spread the 'news'. One leader in particular seemed intent on sticking the knife in good and hard, and started phoning everybody he knew to tell them to remove their support of the Tribe. It was painful, to say the least. It was extraordinary that all we were trying to do was get on with what we were called to do – reach and keep young people and work with God's family across the city – but some members of God's family were too busy trying to undermine our work. Thankfully we were still half-stunned from the powerful way God had spoken to us about Eden, as well as the fact that the partnership with King's Church seemed to be so obviously from God. The church had put all their administration and prayer support behind the project and we simply knew that we had to see it through. If we hadn't been so sure about God's calling, we would have given up on the whole thing long before.

So often this seems to be the pattern followed as the devil gets us from within, killing new things at birth. The devil must have hated the idea of these inner-city strongholds coming to life, and as we saw it as an attack, we moved on with even more determination. We wrote to all the churches in Manchester, explaining things from our side, and launched the idea of recruiting people at the 1997 Soul Survivor summer festival.

As people at home slowly came back around to the idea of supporting Eden, there were more encouragements to come at Soul Survivor. On the afternoon that I was due to introduce the idea to the festival, I was talking to Phil Wall from the Salvation Army missions team.

I had been telling Phil about how I was going to invite people to pack up and move to Wythenshawe, to get their hands dirty and not take the soft option. We wanted between 30 and 40 Christians to move in and make a huge impact on the lives of the local kids. That evening, just before I went up to speak, Phil grabbed me and told me how he believed that God was going to give us a Gideon's army, 300 people for the inner city of Manchester. I had never thought of getting that many people, and I went onto the stage hugely excited and preached my heart out, challenging the young people to move into Manchester.

Hundreds of them volunteered, and out of them 30 moved into Wythenshawe over the next few months. Soon we started pumping young people into King's Church and bit by bit the church started to grow as young people started coming to faith. We haven't seen full-blown revival yet in Wythenshawe, but a vibrant church has grown that reaches out into every area of the community, crime has come down and the atmosphere there has totally changed, no question about it. I believed that it was right to strike the rock, to move people into the toughest place, so the first 20 Eden workers moved into Benchill. The atmosphere there now is undeniably different, and while there is still violence and vandalism, it is no way nearly as intense. Bit by bit God's kingdom is coming to Manchester, and within a year King's Church had grown by about four or five times. Not only that, but there was phenomenal growth going on in both the Planet Life meetings and local school Christian groups. The Eden team was soon having contact with hundreds of kids right across Wythenshawe by working in schools and hanging out on the streets. Finally we began to get a glimpse of how it could all work: not only did King's Church grow, but the other churches right across the estate started to catch the vibe.

Of course any team needs a leader, and Eden was no exception. Because it was something we were so keen on, and because we thought it could well end up being one of the toughest jobs ever, we had fairly fixed ideas about what sort of person we were looking for to take it on. Obviously they would need to have had plenty of experience working as a leader or a manager and would certainly be well into their twenties. Some sort of background of working with young people in an inner-city environment would also be up there on the list of requirements. We started talking with loads of people we thought fitted neatly into the 'key youth leader' box, some who approached us and some whom we approached ourselves. These chats yielded nothing; either we had reservations about them or they didn't fancy taking it on. Many had families to consider, and for some of them the thought of bringing up their children in one of the toughest estates in Britain was, to put it mildly, not very appealing. We fully understood, but were still left in the awkward situation of our most ambitious project so far being without a leader.

As we talked and prayed about it all, one name cropped up more than most. Mark Smethurst was a 19-

year-old lad who had been among the first wave of project workers to move into the area. Like the others he had to work during the week and spend evenings and weekends hanging out with the locals and clearing up the glass after the almost daily attempts to steal his car. Despite his age and lack of 'key youth leader' status, we started to think that he could be the ideal man for the job. He was flexible, keen to learn and able to cope with discouragements, of which there would be many. Within a few weeks of him joining us on the project he accepted the job of leading it, and turned out to be one of our very best workers.

Through Mark God gave us another technicolour example of how He loves to turn things upside down. While we were busy looking for someone with kudos and a publicly recognised track record, He was waving the answer right under our noses. Who else but God would have suggested putting a 19-year-old in charge of a team of 30 people all working in a pressure-cooker environment? It seemed foolish, but it was also brilliant and totally in line with the way God works. He loves to turn things on their head; like getting a scruffy bunch of young Christians involved in breathing some life back into schools and downbeat areas, or choosing screw-ups like you and me to spend the rest of eternity with Him in heaven.

As soon as it was clear that Eden was working in Wythenshawe I started wondering whether we could reproduce it across Manchester. Could this be an answer to the problems of so many of the other spiritual wastelands? Could it be that eventually there would be so many Eden projects going on that the Tribe only ever did missions alongside them? An idea slowly emerged, crazy as all the others, but just as exciting. We wanted to set up ten Eden projects across Manchester, and with thirty working in each one, it really would be a Gideon's army. I called a meeting in Birmingham with some friends from various key youth organisations, and asked if they had the resources to put into Manchester and the desire to work in partnership. Youth for Christ and Salvation Army missions both said that, yes, they did believe God was speaking to them. And so these organisations spent the first half of 1999 sorting out the fine details and recruiting workers together.

I also met with Laurence Singlehurst, the main man at YWAM, who also writes about cell church and has a real heart to disciple inner-city kids. I asked if he knew of anyone who had experience of discipling large numbers of young people like those who were starting to come through Eden. Laurence's comment was, 'Well, William Booth did it,' and neither of us could think of anyone since who had seen big-time breakthrough with inner-city young people. The truth is that there are lots of faithful youth workers in the inner city, but no one is seeing the breakthrough that we are working for in Manchester.

As far as I'm concerned, praying for Eden is like praying for nothing else. It feels as though, as you pray for the inner-city poor and the lost, you touch on God's heart. Jesus was incredibly hard with religious people and yet incredibly gentle with the worst of sinners. He was often accused of hanging out with tax collectors and sinners, but His answer was always, 'It is not the healthy who need a doctor but the sick.' I believe that it is time for the church to start focusing its energies, its efforts and its prayers on the sick. It's time to watch God bring those rivers into the desert. For many that will mean more than just praying and giving; it will mean moving in long term and changing the course of their life. This is the same spirit in which Robert Hawthorne moved a hunded years ago. His was a one-way ticket for the gospel, for the lost. I honestly believe that of all the things I have been involved in, there is nothing more important than Eden. If we can get it right and pull in more partners who want to do similar things right across Britain, the implications are massive. Perhaps, just as things spread out from one tiny church in Wythenshawe, things could spread out from our one small corner of England and start to have an impact on the whole nation.

8

God's Ambush

My friend the wonderful Wallace Benn, who was mentioned in an earlier chapter, was recently consecrated as a bishop in the Church of England and I was invited to the service in London. To be fair it was a fantastic show as bishop after bishop from all over the world paraded in ever more outrageous costumes and got involved in much genuflecting and kissing of Bibles. When it was time for the main attraction, the arrival of the Archbishop of Canterbury, I don't think I would have been surprised to see him enter on a rocket-powered throne.

As much as it was an enjoyable piece of pomp and ceremony, I was also left with a slightly unsettled feeling inside. Just how far from our founder could we as a church possibly get? In some ways it's easy to despair of the Church of England, yet as someone who has spent all of his Christian life in the church, I have been particularly excited to see over the last few years that God hasn't given up on it. Far from trashing it, He has blessed it and used it to encourage people all over the country. His methods were typically unusual, as just when people like me were mouthing off about how the poor churches would get things going, He picked out two posh southerners to have a worldwide influence. First up was the London church with the nicest carpets in the whole country, Holy Trinity Brompton. Their Alpha course (which in some ways is not unlike a souped-up confirmation course) has had a colossal impact in many different countries, introducing thousands to Jesus in a way that almost anyone can follow. What's more, this has all happened in a very short space of time. I am sure that it has God's seal of approval and, with that in place, nothing can stand in its way.

I also believe that God is blessing us all through a church right at the heart of middle-class England. Chorleywood used to be known as the town with the highest number of cars per household, but now the word is out about an offshoot of its youth work. Two top blokes – Mike Pilavachi and Matt Redman – helped to start Soul Survivor in 1992. We got involved once it had been going for a few years, and I remember that on our first visit I immediately got on with Mike, a big-hearted man for Jesus. There are times when I feel that he 'wings it', and occasionally it looks as if Soul Survivor is held together with sticking-plaster, but God is all over the event, the church that came out of it and Mike, the bearded wonder, himself. Everything he touches turns spiritually to gold. That's the kind of person I want to partner with. God's favour is resting on Soul Survivor and it is clear that Matt Redman and other Soul Survivor worship leaders such as Tim Hughes, Martyn Layzell and co have blessed the church in the last few years with worship songs like nobody else. Of course the key has not been down to young guys who write great songs or slightly older guys who preach quite well, like Nicky Gumbel or Mike Pilavachi. It's obviously down to the Lord's favour.

I was recently at a prayer meeting with New Generation Ministries in Bristol. Danny Budd, one of their leaders, started praying for me and quoted that verse from 2 Chronicles 16 where the Bible says, 'The eyes of the Lord range throughout the earth to strengthen those whose hearts are fully committed to him' (v. 9). I felt massively challenged. Could I be called a man whose heart was fully after God's? Because, if I could, the Lord Himself would strengthen what we've been trying to do in Manchester, and when He strengthens something you know about it.

Well, it's obvious to me that the Lord's eyes have rested on Holy Trinity Brompton, particularly on Nicky Gumbel and co. Because He's seen their hearts, He's exploded what they (and also what Mike, Tim, Matt and the others at Soul Survivor) have done.

The really wonderful thing about that verse is that the Lord isn't looking for gifting – just a heart. There's a promise that goes with it too: when He finds that heart, the man or woman attached to it will be strongly supported by Him.

It was on our first visit to the festival that I spent a bit of time with Mike and realised just why God supported Soul Survivor. We found that God was saying the same thing to our two ministries: that combining young people with a radical relationship with Jesus is a recipe for huge change. Being one of those people who go out of their way to encourage the things they believe in, over the years Mike gave us more and more room at the events to get our message heard. When we had the idea for Eden Mike wanted us to use the event in any way we could to help launch the project. We had an incredible intercession afternoon when all the seminars were closed and thousands of young people got together just to pray for Manchester and Eden. Mike gave me a preaching slot on the main stage, and everywhere he went he was talking about Eden and the work of the Tribe in Manchester. Needless to say, I liked the guy.

We were both at Spring Harvest together in 1997; the Tribe were leading the youth venue and Mike was doing something with the older ones. He and I went for a coffee with Matt Redman and Cameron, and sat around half-expecting it to be one of those chats where we did a bit of networking, had a laugh and compared stories of feeling too old for youth work. God, it appeared, had other plans. He ambushed our cosy chat and changed everything.

We started talking about Manchester, Eden and some of the things that were going on at the time. I was telling them about my dreams for a big mission in the city, and explaining how we were already sensing that Manchester was ripe for a large-scale move of God. The year before, Mike had put us in touch with a German guy called Roland Werner, who was organising a city-wide mission in Dresden called 'Christival'. It was an event that had exploded and grown beyond their wildest dreams. Having started out praying for 10,000 to come along, they ended up getting 35,000 Christians who wanted to be involved, and even had to turn 20,000 away. There were 13 venues across the city, all rammed full with a variety of evangelistic events. The idea was that the Christians spent the afternoons out on the streets, witnessing and bringing people along to the evening meetings. Literally hundreds were becoming Christians each day, and for one week Dresden was taken over by the gospel. There were helium balloons on the corner of every street saying 'Come follow Jesus' and posters all over the city invited people along to the evening events. The Tribe had been doing a few gigs and none of us who went had ever seen anything like it. Chatting with Mike, Cam and Matt, I started going on about how wonderful it would be if we could do something like that in Manchester, getting thousands of Christians on board to really blitz the city.

A few days later Mike phoned me up. I could tell that he was excited by the way he was shouting and not letting me get a word in. Slowly I managed to piece together what he was saying: he had a mad idea to cancel the Soul Survivor festival for the year 2000. Instead of having it in the usual field in Somerset he

wanted to move it and the 20,000 punters up to
Manchester for two five-day missions. In the morning
they could meet for Soul Survivor-style worship, teaching and ministry in the Holy Spirit, and in the afternoons
they could get out onto the streets and start meeting
people to bring along to the venues for evening events
across the city. Of course this took my breath away, and
any plans for a mission I had previously been working
on were blown out of the water. I'd been thinking about
the possibility of hiring the Manchester Arena for one or
two nights in the year 2000, but Mike was suggesting
booking not just that venue, but every other place available for ten nights running.

I realised that through Soul Survivor's resources we
could do this. We had a meeting and started to talk
about how we worked on the Message '88, laying the
foundation of getting support from the local churches.
Back then we had 300 churches behind us, and we were
sure we could do it again. We suggested that we would
be able to set up an office and spend two years working
on 'the ramp-up'; building support and making sure
that the biggest youth mission ever attempted in the UK
would have plenty of churches ready to pastor the influx
of new Christians.

Without really realising what the implications would
be and just how complicated it could all get, we both
agreed to go for it and publicly work together. We
started pulling in partners: Youth for Christ to look after
all the street work for the big event and Oasis to take on
board the social action work. We wanted social action to

be right at the heart of this thing, and we wanted to present a holistic gospel; not just to beat people over the head with a Bible, but to meet their real needs. We decided that 60 per cent of the delegates should be working on up-front evangelistic work and 40 per cent should be involved in social action right across the city. Quickly plans began to develop; we could establish and maintain some sort of a homeless project, we could paint hundreds of houses on the estates and clean up neglected areas.

At Soul Survivor 1997 Mike announced the plans and they were greeted with a standing ovation. The whole festival was buzzing about Soul Survivor – The Message 2000. It was fantastic to see so many people who were up for it, and to think that so many young Christians would be coming over to Manchester for the mission. It was like the wildest dream slowly becoming a reality, and at times it seemed too good to be true.

Returning from the summer festivals we knew that we couldn't leave Soul Survivor holding the baby. It was our city, in that we were based there and had the initial contacts, so we got on with the business of setting up the office and recruiting a team. The local churches were our main targets and we had learnt a fair bit about working alongside them from the previous six years. We had found out how vital it was that the churches we wanted to support us were given plenty of training, resources and opportunities to get involved with missions. They also had to be allowed to learn from their own mistakes and add their own unique flavouring to the events. From the start, Soul Survivor – The Message 2000 was seen not as a stand-alone event, but as a climax of a whole year that would be stuffed full of missions and outreaches. Throughout the twelve months that led up to the event there would be over 500 local missions going on and over 100 social action projects being identified and prepared for. That way, when the thousands of workers arrived, much of the city would be ripe for the gospel. Mike Breen, a vicar from Sheffield, told me how he believed people would write about the events of Message 2000 in centuries to come and describe them as a big move of God. Living with it day by day it often didn't feel much like a move of God. Sometimes the work we do feels more like throwing mud against a wall, seeing a few people become Christians and seeing life break out slowly. But the church in Manchester is not the same as it was when I first became a Christian. The prayer movement in this city is significant, and the number of people coming to faith, their fire and passion, should be enough to convince anyone that something is going on. We want to milk that for Jesus' glory; we want to see a city turned around. We don't just want to see a few people come to faith; we want to see a large region changed, not for the glory of any organisation but for the glory of Jesus, the only one who deserves it.

Tied in with this dream that seemed to be becoming a reality was an even crazier idea. If we could do this in Manchester, drawing in people from all over the world to see what we have done, maybe they would want to do it in their cities. While we get on with following up and keeping all the young people who come to faith perhaps others will target big cities worldwide for something similar. Could it be that the pattern of a year of local church mission and activity, prayer and preparation, culminating in thousands upon thousands of Christians getting stuck into an intense mission would work elsewhere? If it could, and if people were committed to targeting the toughest and poorest areas, then just imagine the impact they could have. That's what Soul Survivor – The Message 2000 was all about: us trying to fulfil our calling to see every young person in Manchester being given repeated opportunities to accept or reject Jesus. That is the goal that we will continue to chase, heads down, until we can put our hands on our hearts and say that it has happened.

One of the best decisions we made in the early years was to spend one day each month away from the schools and the offices. This wasn't an excuse to bunk off, but a chance to spend valuable time praying and checking with God that we were keeping on the right track. We have always wanted to do our best to fulfil the calling that He has for us and have known for a long time that prayer is a vital part of making sure that it happens.

These have consistently been great times, and through them I have developed a theory on prayer. I'm convinced that it takes time to really hear from God. Often when we start praying we are so weighed down by excess baggage and surrounded by so much rubbish that it takes more than a few minutes to really break through and touch the heart of God.

Prayer can often seem like wading through mud. For ages it can seem as if God's on holiday and that nothing can bring Him back. But suddenly all that can change, and you find yourself right in there hearing from God and receiving direction. We've been through this loads of times, and it's definitely been the case that most of our good ideas have started during the times of revelation that follow the hard slog.

We had one particularly memorable day early on in 1997. My friend Frank Green was praying for me when God powerfully touched me and knocked me right off my feet. I was left on the floor feeling decidedly un-Anglican, when a clear picture came into my mind. It was of a circular saw spinning at great speed. As I looked, I could see logs falling into a basket by the side. I felt as though God were saying, 'It's good what you've been doing with the Message, and you've actually been cutting through a bit, but it's been hard work. Pretty soon My power is going to kick in and the whole thing is going to speed up to such an extent that no one could ever say it was through human efforts.' All I could think was, 'Bring it on, God!'

9

Life is a Roller Coaster

As things moved on at a pace towards Soul Survivor – The Message 2000, I found myself living with what I can only describe as increased tension. Inside I was a mess of conflict between faith and fact. On one hand I was feeling as if we were on the verge of full-blown Holy Spirit revival, with vision coming out of our earholes, then on the other hand there were the bleaker times. Funnily enough these usually coincided with one of our regular cashflow crises or when I became too focused on the work of the Lord rather than the Lord of the work. More than once I felt like throwing it all in and going back to selling braces for a living.

I put these thoughts into words and sent them off to my elder brother Michael. He's doing heroic work in India caring for orphaned children and teaching English to the poorest of the poor in a school out there. I described our life in Manchester as a roller coaster.

This is what he wrote in reply:

> It seems to me that a life of any purpose on the earth is likely to be a roller coaster; the only difference being a Christian is that it's a wilder ride, having a spiritual dimension as well (eat your heart out, Alton Towers). As you imply *viz-a-viz* selling braces, the only alternative life on offer (for now) would be one of those little kiddie rides you can also get at the fairground, where you sit on the tiny pointless train and go round and round. This, one has to admit, can seem quite pleasant from time to time, and maybe the Lord in His grace will offer you such an interval whilst He stands lovingly watching you trundle by waving, holding your baggage and of course paying for the ride. But, like all His children, I suspect you are the sort who quickly gets bored.

How true is that? I've got a feeling that as we really move on in God's purposes the ride will get even bumpier, with greater highs and even tougher lows. But were we ever promised anything different? I know one thing for sure: I wouldn't want to be on any other ride.

One of the new ideas we launched at the start of 2000 was the Eden Bus ministry. We weren't the first to guess that asking people to come and meet God in a funny religious building is a strange way of going about things. Getting on a bus that turns up on your doorstep is, well, as easy as getting on a bus. It can go right into the heart of the tough places with the good news. It also has the added advantage of being able to leg it quickly if things get a bit hot. By early 2000 we had

Eden projects in Wythenshawe and Salford and were gearing up to launch a couple more in Openshaw and Longsight on the back of Message 2000. It seemed that a mobile youth centre could be a brilliant resource for those guys as they tried to get alongside the young people in these tough estates.

Unlike most of the bangers Christians use for this sort of ministry, we wanted our Eden Bus to be really excellent, with the latest sound system, video presentation facility and games machines. We set a cool Christian architect the job of coming up with something that would really blow the young people on the Eden projects away. The only problem, as I'm sure you can imagine, was that such things don't come cheap.

In the build-up to Message 2000 we had a big dinner at Old Trafford football ground. Now, being a Manchester United supporter, I personally find this a very conducive place for dreaming dreams, and I was hoping the others would get the buzz. We'd invited various business people and gave them the vision for Soul Survivor – The Message 2000. We also took the opportunity to share with them some of our dreams to shift the ministry up a gear after the event, with new Eden projects, LifeCentres and the bus ministry.

I had just done my bit and finished the evening with a prayer when one of our guests asked if he could say something. His little speech went something like this: 'I'm a little ashamed to say this, but it's my wife's birthday today and I've forgotten to buy her a present. While you were talking I thought I'd like to buy her a bus for her birthday – not just any bus, but a bus that can go into the inner city and reach young people with the love of Jesus.' And with that he sat down.

His forgetfulness had proved more than a little expensive. Not only did he agree there and then to pay all the purchase and refurbishment costs of the amazing Eden Bus 1, but he also phoned the next day to tell us he wanted to cover all the salaries and the extra costs that went with running this new ministry. We were more than a little excited, and shortly found ourselves a bus and started doing it up to a spec that would set a new standard in terms of bus work.

But there was one problem. Now we had this fantastic new bus, but no one to run it. I went away to the Soul Survivor summer festival needing a team leader for this new ministry right away. It was right at the top of my prayer list and in my head all the time, even while I was leading seminars with the Tribe to train and prepare people for Message 2000. At the end of one of these meetings a guy called John came up to me. He was a guy with a serious set of tattoos, and, as often happens, he asked me if there was any chance of the Tribe coming to do a gig for him in Southampton. However, there was something about this conversation that felt different. As I looked at him all I could think was, 'Here is the man to head up our new bus ministry.' So, rather feebly, I asked him, 'You don't drive a bus, do you?'

He looked at me as if I were a bit weird and asked me to explain myself. As I told him about the bus ministry his eyes lit up. He was working in inner-city Southampton, driving vans into the toughest areas to reach out for Jesus, yet both he and his wife (who is a Church of England curate) had felt it was time for a change and had been seeking God for what was next.

I don't specialise in words of knowledge, but that afternoon I knew we had our man. I'm aware that it's probably not best recruitment practice, but what can you do? By the end of Soul Survivor we'd offered him the job, and a few weeks later he moved to Manchester with his wife and two kids to start a new life. It has proved to be quite literally an inspired choice. You can read John's full and amazing story in his book *Nobody's Child*, but in short John Robinson had the least promising start in life. He had eleven brothers and sisters, a violent father and an alcoholic mother. Very early on, all the children were taken into care and moved from one abusive foster parent to the next. He went through the cycle that so often accompanies young people who have had a bad deal in life: violence, crime, borstal and eventually prison. After that he was jobless and homeless, and spent seven years on the streets.

One day, while he was living rough, a big guy with a skinhead approached John and said to him, 'Jesus loves you.' Right then and at that particular point in his life John felt extremely *un*loved, but there was something about this guy that made him stop and listen. The skinhead invited him to go and hear a preacher called Clive Calver. Now Clive's a fantastic bloke and a top communicator, but hardly my idea of an evangelist to the homeless. During his talk he pointed at the audience and told them all to take off their dirty clothes and give them to God. At first John was pretty embarrassed and offended, but then it began to make sense. God was telling him to take off the dirty clothes of misery, pain, rejection, anger, a sense of betrayal and loneliness, and put on new clothes of freedom, forgiveness and peace. He closed his eyes and prayed, asked Jesus to come into his life and forgive him, and then started to bawl his eyes out. He said later that he felt as if a heavy rucksack had been taken off his shoulders. For the first time in his life he felt as if he was really loved and special.

The skinhead didn't just invite him to that one meeting; the next day he invited John to live with him and his wife. For the next two years Tony and Sylvia worked through a whole load of issues and problems with John as he embarked on his new life of faith.

John eventually went to college, got a professional youth work qualification, met and married his wife Gillian – now a Church of England vicar – and started his amazing work to the toughest young people of Southampton.

I'm sure it has a lot to do with his background, but I don't think I've ever met anyone with such a big heart for damaged, dysfunctional young people as John. I absolutely love the regular phone calls I get from him whenever someone commits their life to Jesus on the bus. He gets so excited because he knows this wonderful gospel really does work like nothing else, even in the most broken lives and the most damaged communities.

Today we have *two* superb high-tech buses working

in the toughest communities of Manchester alongside Eden teams of dedicated youth workers letting their lights shine in the darkness. And all because some guy forgot his wife's birthday. God bless amnesia.

In so many ways John is a huge encouragement to us at the Message, not only because he's a lot of fun to have around and has a passionate evangelist's heart, but because he reminds us daily that God really can take the most broken people and transform them and then use them for His glory. Often when we see drug addicts, alcoholics or young people who are involved in gang culture come to faith, the worry is that they might not make a go of it. But the good news is that our God doesn't just start things; He's good at finishing them too. I love that famous verse in Philippians 1 where Paul says of his new converts: 'Being confident of this, that he who began a good work in you will carry it on to completion . . .' (v. 6).

Isn't that great? God is good at saving people and He's good at keeping them saved. We should do everything we can to help, encourage and pray for baby Christians, especially the ones who could be described as 'premature'. This is exactly the type we're seeing become Christians: the ones who need lots of special care and attention, just like the care and attention Tony and Sylvia gave to John. But it's good to know that the real work of keeping people going is down to the Holy Spirit – and He is better at it than we are.

In Ephesians 2, the Bible talks about our new life in Christ and says that because of His great love for us God 'raised us up with Christ and seated us with him in the heavenly realms' (v. 6). That means that just as Jesus is seated on a throne ruling and reigning, so are you, I, John Robinson and all the other weird and wonderful people who come to know Jesus. When you meet Him, you go from the bottom of hell to the top of heaven in an instant. When God seats you with Christ to share His inheritance with you, He tends to superglue your backside to that throne for all eternity. Once we're saved we're saved, and nothing can change that. It's important to know that our salvation isn't based on our efforts and that no amount of going around schools rapping for Jesus could make me good enough for heaven. It's completely based on what He did for us on the cross. As followers of Jesus, however, we have a massive responsibility to grow up in Jesus and to give it everything we've got in response to His amazing love.

I like a story I heard about J. C. Ryle, who was Bishop of Liverpool in the Church of England at the end of the nineteenth century. These were the days when the Salvation Army was exploding with life, and J. C. Ryle was approached on a train by a zealous young Salvation Army girl. She'd seen his dog collar and obviously thought he couldn't possibly be a real Christian as she asked him if he were saved. J. C.'s answer was brilliant: 'Well, it depends what you mean by being "saved", sister. You could say I'm drowning in a lake and somebody throws me a lifebelt and I'm saved. However, you could say I climb into the boat and am rowing for shore and I'm saved. On the other hand, you could say I'm safely back on the shore and I'm saved.' He paused for a moment and then said, 'I think I'm in the boat, sister.'

It's clear from the Bible that there's getting saved – a God thing that happens every time a young scally surrenders their life to Jesus in a Manchester school – but there's also the business of daily being saved from our sins as we row towards the shore and bit by bit we see the rubbish in our lives being dealt with. That cool stuff happens only as we co-operate with God and decide to grow, make an effort to grow and keep on growing day by day, or stroke by stroke if you like.

Then of course there's the ultimate being saved, in heaven, safe on the shore for all eternity. It's at that point that I'm sure a lot of us will think, 'It's so amazing here, but I do wish I'd rowed that bit harder while I had the chance.'

10

Seeing is Believing

At the start of the year 2000, things began to hot up. Ahead of us lay what would become the largest youth mission ever attempted in the UK. We had our local team in place to ramp up the churches and prepare quality projects for the delegates to work on. For their part, Soul Survivor were focusing most of their efforts on recruiting the thousands of young people we planned to have working on the streets of Manchester. All in all, it was quite an operation.

Once again God stunned us with the quality of people He called to be involved – like Andrew Belfield. He was a pastor at one of the largest churches in Britain and had been on the receiving end of some divine instructions. He had a strong sense that he ought to move from his home in Nottingham to Manchester. So he announced it to the church and moved with his wife Ruth and their three kids, but without any idea of what he might do once he got here. Actually, he did have a couple of names of people to get in touch with given to him by his friend J. John. One of the contacts happened to be Val Grieve, the guy we had spoken to right at the start of the Message adventures. The other one was me.

Andrew went to see Val and talked about how they might work together, but a couple of days later Val died suddenly. I don't know why, but this often seems to be the way it happens with amazing men and women of God: the end is swift and unexpected. Still, it wasn't a great start to Andrew's Manchester move, so falling back on his only other contact in the area he called me up. As soon as I met Andrew I felt we had our man, especially as he kept telling me he didn't want paying. So we took Andrew on to head up our Message 2000 Manchester team and he proved to be a magnet for the most amazingly committed and gifted staff and volunteers. He pulled them all together to see the whole thing through.

Working alongside Andrew was Matt Wilson. Matt is as sharp as nails, has a first class honours degree and had been getting his career going at a local design studio. However, he agreed to take a break from his career to pitch in with Message 2000 for a couple of years.

Matt hadn't been with us for very long before I started thinking that I couldn't bear to lose this guy back into the design industry after Message 2000. Maybe, I hoped, God had a path for Matt that, although perhaps less financially rewarding, would

ultimately involve the biggest buzz in the world: seeing loads of people impacted for Jesus through his work.

For some time we had thought it would be a good
idea to set up a training school in Manchester to
mobilise and equip young people, and allow them to
get hands-on experience with all the good stuff that
was happening across the city. As I prayed, it became
obvious to me that Matt was the man for the job, and I
was keen to get on with it. Unfortunately, Matt wasn't
quite as impressed with the whole idea as I'd hoped. He
promised to go away and pray about it and approxi-
mately a week later he sent me a long letter explaining
that something weird had happened to him. Good stuff,
I thought. At 3 a.m. the previous morning he'd woken
up and God had filled his mind with ideas for the
school. 'It should be an evangelists' training school,' his
letter said. 'That's our distinctive – our characteristic.
Let's identify radical young guys and girls and train
them in knowledge, character, skills and motivation, but
most of all train and equip them to be soul winners.'

I liked it. I loved it. And I couldn't believe Matt was
dilly-dallying about whether he was the man to head it
up. We agreed to talk again a week later in Norwich at
the Pioneer conference where we were both planning to
bang the drum about Message 2000. Matt suggested
that we pray about it some more but not tell anyone
just yet.

At the Pioneer conference a couple of bizarre things
happened. First, Gerald Coates pulled me out and
prayed for me while pouring a five-litre bottle of water

over my head. Secondly, on Gerald's instruction, I was lifted up by a group of men above the 4,000-strong congregation. I was not only wet through but feeling like a right idiot high above the crowd when one of Gerald's co-workers, Martin Scott, started to prophesy over me. It went something like this: 'You haven't told anyone about this yet, but it is on your heart to set up a training school in Manchester for young believers who will come to Manchester for five or six months to be trained and catch a vision for what you do and then be sent all over the world to bring in the harvest. Press on with this idea because it is from the Lord and will be very fruitful.'

Martin Scott had no idea that we were just about to have a meeting to discuss this very thing. Matt was standing about ten feet down and two feet across from me, and by the look on his face I could see that God had nailed him!

We launched Xcelerate – the evangelist training school – on the back of Message 2000. Since then loads of young people have gone through the course and many, just like Martin Scott prophesied, have gone all over the world, including those who have joined our Eden projects and had great adventures for Jesus.

After the Pioneer conference, however, Matt didn't have a lot of time to think about Xcelerate. His days and nights were filled with the small task of identifying and co-ordinating the 400 projects across the city that the young people would work on. Despite doing a brilliant job, we were still short of work for about a thousand delegates with six weeks to go. In desperation I spoke to a police officer friend of mine, Phil Gleave, and asked him if there was any way the police could usefully use a thousand fired-up Christians as part of Message 2000.

It's a good thing that Phil loves a challenge. Within a couple of days he had come up with a plan to put all thousand of them to work on a notorious estate in Swinton called the Valley. The Valley was a real crime black spot, one which was known locally as the Bronx. Local taxi drivers refused to take you onto the estate because of the intimidating atmosphere. You get the picture. Phil had ambitious plans for what they could do over the ten days: totally clean up the estate, work on hundreds of gardens and create a community garden and a dog-walking track, as well as refurbish the run-down community and resource centres. It sounded like a massive task, especially as Phil told us he didn't have any money. But when we went to see the Valley and looked at the rows and rows of boarded-up houses and saw the rubbish strewn along the streets, we got some sense of the desperation of the people who lived there. We knew we had to do something.

Prophecy, particularly the type where a normal man will predict the future and claim to be the mouthpiece of God, is a funny old gift. Like most of the gifts of the Spirit it is incredibly open to abuse. The Bible, however, commands us in 1 Thessalonians 5 not to 'treat prophecies with contempt. Test everything. Hold on to the good' (vv. 19–21). In the build-up to Message 2000 we had another cracker.

Dave Connolly helps to lead one of my favourite churches anywhere: the Frontline Centre in inner-city Liverpool. He, like Martin Scott, is a pretty awesome prophet. A couple of weeks after my meeting with Phil he came to see me. Among other things, he prophesied that I was about to come face to face with things that I would have to see to believe. Looking back now it's crystal clear that he was talking about what went on in Swinton Valley that summer.

There was a tangible sense of God's presence as the delegates took to the massive task. To walk round the estate and see hardened criminals working alongside the delegates for the good of their community was something else. Worship songs seemed to be wafting from every corner and as well as lots of people becoming Christians, all sorts of relationships, some that had been broken for generations, were restored. It really did feel like the nearest thing to revival I have ever experienced.

During those ten days there were no recorded incidents of crime on that whole estate and since then there has been a sustained 43 per cent reduction in crime. All the boarded-up houses have now gone and it's a struggle to get a house on the Valley as people actually want to move into an area that has had a dose of God's goodness.

On the final night of Soul Survivor – The Message, 2000 loads of the residents came to the big evangelistic bash that happened every night at the arena. They brought with them a great big bucket of money that they had collected off their own bat from around the estate for the mission. This was from an estate where the vast majority of the people were out of work for one reason or another. A non-Christian police officer also stood up to thank us and said, 'Question: How do you get zero crime on one of Manchester's toughest estates? Answer: Move a thousand Christians in.' You really did have to see it to believe it. On the back of Soul Survivor – The Message 2000, a vibrant church has been planted, an Eden project has been established and God continues to do good things in the area.

But this is moving on too fast. The other thing that happened with only six weeks to go before the mission kicked off was Mike Pilavachi. To be more precise it was Mike Pilavachi's nerves that happened, as he started to get extremely flappy about the budget. I couldn't blame him, especially as the delegate numbers, which were a pretty key part of the budget, just weren't coming in as we'd all hoped. Mike started to write articles along the lines of 'By the time you read this Soul Survivor will be out of business, but better to have tried and failed than to have not tried at all . . .'. He also told me later that when the full financial disaster hit, as he was sure it eventually would, his plan was to go to his favourite place in the world, Durban, South Africa, and set up a beach bar. Fortunately, God had other ideas for him and for the mission itself.

Once again the Lord bailed us out big time through His people. Not only did the delegates give an incredible £112,000 in the offering (on top of their delegate fees), but lots of Christian businessmen stood with us, including one who gave us £125,000 – the largest gift we'd ever had. It really was flying by the seat of our pants time. For ages I'd been teaching that if you're not in a place where you're absolutely stuffed without God then you ought to get there. Message 2000 definitely took both our ministries to that place. And beyond.

For me the other highlight of the mission was the final morning. Every day before had started with us all meeting in the main arena for worship, teaching and ministry, Soul Survivor-style. After that we'd sent the delegates out across the city to do their fantastic work on the hundreds of projects that were running. On the final morning, Mike invited people to give a testimony to what God had been doing. People came forward with the most amazing stories of healing and salvation happening all over the city. One of the last to speak was Anna, one of our Eden workers in Wythenshawe, a bright spark who was offered a top job with the United Nations in London, but instead chose to move into an area that was officially the poorest in Britain. I knew what a price she had paid over the past three years to make Jesus known and to see that community changed. She told of the amazing atmosphere in Wythenshawe during the ten days and of all the young people coming to faith and travelling home singing worship songs at the top of their voices. What really did me in, though, was when she told of Johnny, a heroin addict who had given his life to the Lord at the start of the mission, and had gone on to lead his pregnant girlfriend to the Lord.

Anna said, '. . . and now that baby will be brought up in a Jesus-filled home.' I'm not an emotional man – in fact my wife gets very frustrated that I don't cry very much at all, especially when she will be bawling away at the latest trauma in *Coronation Street*. That morning, however, as I rejoiced over what a wonderful thing Jesus had done across Manchester, I cried my eyes out.

Mike Pilavachi had been keen that social action would be a core element of Message 2000. For me, with my conservative evangelical background where preaching the word is everything, I found myself feeling a little uncomfortable. The big question for me was, 'Is doing people's gardens and removing graffiti from outside their houses and the like really evangelism, or would the thousands of young people be better employed preaching the gospel on street corners?'

Message 2000 convinced me that not only was it right, but that an essential part of Christian mission is to care for the whole person. It makes sense that often, before people are ready to hear the gospel, they need (especially in tough areas) to see the gospel in action. Finally we'd hit on something where we as a church could make people feel good about themselves. This was a big shift along from the model the church had used for generations, where our main aim always seemed to be making people feel bad. To be honest, it's shaped the way we've done our outreach ever since.

It's fascinating that the biggest full-on evangelists of past generations seem to be the ones who were most committed to social action. William Booth, who transformed the inner cities with his social campaign, said to his workers, 'We are a salvation people, this is our speciality; getting saved, keeping saved and getting others saved . . .' John Wesley, who also brought much social reform through his Methodist revival movement, charged his workers with these words: 'You have nothing to do but save souls. Therefore spend and be spent in this great work.'

These guys knew that their top priority was plundering hell and populating heaven. They also knew that social action and evangelism are completely inseparable for the Christian. After all, Jesus summed up His ministry right at the start through the words of Isaiah: 'The Spirit of the Lord is on me, because he has anointed me to preach good news to the poor. He has sent me to proclaim freedom for the prisoners and recovery of sight for the blind' (Luke 4:18).

The same Spirit is on all real Christians everywhere. Imagine if we really allowed Him not just to focus us on either preaching or caring or miracles alone but to be filled and equipped by Him to preach the full gospel in word and deed. Imagine if the church really got out there, not only boldly proclaiming the message but also extravagantly caring for communities and believing for and seeing amazing miracles. How exciting would that be?

The other interesting thing that happened at Message 2000 was that the Tribe mark 3 came to an end. About three months before the mission we had an approach from Gotee records in America. Now this all looked pretty good, especially as I felt they were the coolest Christian label around and would be the ideal new platform for the Tribe in the States. They'd heard *Frantik*, had loved it and wanted to do a distribution deal over there. Best of all, it was all on the table despite the fact that they knew that, as ever with the band, promotion and touring opportunities would be limited due to the focus on our beloved Manchester.

I was excited. I got the guys together and told them the great news about Gotee, confident that they would be as made up as I was. Yet one by one they looked at their boots and said they really felt it was time to leave. Deronda told me that she needed to go back home to the States to be with her daughter. Colette wanted to bury herself in the Wythenshawe Eden project and have babies. Cameron had this massive heart for club culture and Claire said she really needed to go to Bible college and get trained up. They were all brilliant reasons, but I watched the band fall apart before my eyes. We were left with Tim, Emma and new boy Lindsay West, who had joined early in 2000. Understandably Gotee weren't too impressed and suddenly changed their minds about the deal.

It was disappointing. But it was also obvious that Message 2000 would act as a natural and logical conclusion to the World Wide Message Tribe. By now it was clear there would be life after the Tribe as the developing work of the trust included the Eden projects, the bus ministry, LifeCentres, our vision for Xcelerate, Planet Life and lots of other stuff. However, it did feel as if losing our flagship band was a big deal.

Tim Owen had by now taken over the artistic direction of the band and had become very friendly with a South African band called MIC, through doing various gigs together. Once a year they would come over for a few months and pitch in and help us with our work in Manchester. We had grown to love them and been really impressed, not just with their gifts, but with their whole attitude and desire to serve what we were doing. With the future of the band so uncertain (in fact, it had got to the point where we thought it was 'game over' for the Tribe), Tim, Emma and Lindsay met up with George and Quintin from MIC, who had a bit of news to pass on. The two South Africans told our lot that they really thought it was time to leave MIC. The only thing was, they weren't sure what God had for them next. Tim's ears pricked up and he started to dream dreams about yet another Tribe, with the two MIC boys at the heart of it. They were both top singers and songwriters and had a huge desire to be used by God. So it was to my delighted surprise that the Tribe mark 4 was launched on the back of Message 2000. It was also decided that along with the new line-up, new sound and new image we should also change the name. By now most people were calling the World Wide Message Tribe the Tribe anyway, so we decided to make it official in the autumn of 2000.

It's my belief that George and Quintin's arrival has taken the whole thing up to another level. They have been instrumental in the band coming up with two more cracking albums – *Take Back the Beat* and *Raise Your Game* – plus our key discipleship resource *Fresh*. In fact, over the last three years, everything has shifted up a gear, and the Tribe has even had a baby: a healthy girl band called Blush^uk, now also let loose on the streets of Manchester.

Looking back over the various Tribe line-ups it's so encouraging to know that despite various moments of flappiness from me, the Lord really does know what He is doing. Of course He has just the right people waiting in the wings to come forward and partner with us at just the right time so we can fulfil His wonderful purposes for our lives. But I'm sure I'll still flap a little from time to time.

11

The Mopping-Up Operation

The period after Soul Survivor – The Message 2000 was a bit of a strange time for us. We'd put so much effort into it and despite the fact that it felt as if ten years' work had been done in those ten days, and that loads of new ministries were born on the back of it, there was still something of a sense of anti-climax. Full-blown revival hadn't broken out. Yes, God had done some good stuff, but in all honesty the life of the vast majority of Mancunians went on as if nothing had happened.

What were we to do? Press on with more and more of the anonymous servant stuff in the hard places, or stick our necks out and go for something big and city-wide? It wasn't long before the answer came, and of course the answer was both, because as someone cleverer than me pointed out, Jesus' view of the kingdom included both. He described kingdom people as salt and yeast – invisible things where only a tiny bit makes a huge difference (a bit like Eden at its best or the LifeCentres or the buses), but He also compared the kingdom to a 'city on a hill' and 'a great tree that all the birds of the air could gather in' – something big that can't be missed, that grabs the attention. I knew that I wanted us to do more of both these things.

About six weeks after Message 2000, Nigel Gordon, who is European Director of the Luis Palau Evangelistic Association, sent me a video in the post. At exactly the same time as Message 2000 was happening over here, Luis Palau in the States had been modelling something new in Portland, Oregon, called 'Portland Festival'. Now Luis is a totally hardcore evangelist and has preached the gospel in season and out of season for the past 40-odd years. For decades his bread and butter had been campaign evangelism, where thousands would gather in a stadium to hear the gospel preached. But increasingly Luis had become frustrated with how few non-Christians were coming to this type of presentation. Then on one occasion, as he was flying back into his hometown of Portland, he looked down on the waterfront area and had a God-inspired idea. Why not hold a free open-air festival with great bands and entertainment: a kids' area, a skate park, a fun fair, loads of stuff that would bring the whole family out, and right at the heart of it all would be the Christian message? It was an idea that grabbed the attention of the churches and the authorities. That summer well over 100,000 people attended the first Portland Festival and right across the festival area, in the kids' zone, the skate park and in front of the huge main stage, thousands committed their lives to Christ. Since then, this new model has turned the ministry of Luis Palau upside down and hundreds of thousands have attended festivals right across North and South America.

Luis, however, has always had a heart for the UK and asked his man in Europe to try and find suitable partners to pull off a festival here. Nigel Gordon had heard about what we'd done through Soul Survivor – The Message 2000 and so sent us a video to see if we were interested in some sort of partnership.

When I saw the video I was blown away with the sheer scale of the thing, the excellence of it and particularly with the unashamed Jesus-centredness of it all. I was more than interested, so I arranged to meet with Nigel as soon as I could. We discussed a plan where each of us would play to our strengths; we would do everything we could to mobilise young people to serve the city on social action projects, particularly in the deprived areas of Manchester, and on the back of that, they would help us put on a huge weekend party in the park at which Luis would be a keynote speaker.

Once again I went to see the church leaders in Manchester and presented an idea for their approval called Festival:Manchester, desperately hoping they weren't all too exhausted after all the effort of Message 2000 to get their heads round another wacky idea. Fortunately they all seemed well up for it and so early in 2002 we officially launched Festival:Manchester, praying this time for 500 churches to get on board from right across the streams and denominations.

I then went out to Myrtle Beach, North Carolina, to witness a festival first hand. What I saw convinced me all the more that we really were onto something here. I also got to spend quite a bit of time with the great man himself, Luis Palau. As an evangelist, I was really challenged by the way Luis grabbed every opportunity to share his faith, regardless of whether it was one to one or to crowds of tens of thousands. On the Saturday he had the most ridiculous schedule, which went from early morning press conferences right through until after midnight, when he was on the local TV station preaching his heart out. In the afternoon a businessman, who was part of the organising team, asked Luis if he would mind coming to speak to his staff, as he had about a hundred Puerto Rican employees, whom Luis could preach to in Spanish. I know that I would have said that I was just a little on the busy side and would have sent one of my team along instead. But not Luis. The hardcore evangelist that he is saw another opportunity not to be missed and said, 'I'd love to, brother.' He came back about two hours later and I asked him how he had got on.

'Oh, it was wonderful, Andy,' he said. 'Seventy-three were saved!'

After we had said our farewells on the Sunday, we parted. Then Luis came back after me with a final bit of wisdom: 'Andy, don't spend all your time telling Christians how to reach the lost. You get out there.'

It was a good reminder. So often we can let good things get in the way of God's best and I know that as an evangelist God's best for me is reaching people who don't know Jesus – not spending all my time telling others how to do it.

Partnership sounds great in practice, but of course the reality of it is always much harder. I'm sure in the build-up to Festival:Manchester we drove the Luis Palau team up the wall with our tunnel vision on young people and the inner city, and likewise some of the American ways of doing things seemed to us cheesy and so far from where we were at. Like all good partnerships, it took grace and compromise on both sides.

One thing they brought from America that was a first for a UK church mission (as far as I know) was the corporate sponsorship model. The idea is simple: businesses invest in the mission and get to stick their logos all over the place. There were a few raised eyebrows as to whether this would work and whether it would seem as though we were selling out, but we believed that if we could get household names sponsoring the event we would be well on the way to convincing the city that this wasn't just some little Christian jamboree but a serious, credible festival, right up there with anything the world could put on. We ended up with sponsors such as Shell, Lookers, Irn Bru, Friends Provident, B&Q, KPMG and Yorkshire Bank splattered all over our publicity and the delegate T-shirts.

We were also determined to get some major mainstream artists to headline at the event in order to pull in the punters so we could then sock it to them about Jesus. This bit, however, didn't work. No matter how hard we tried and how much money we offered, we just couldn't get a household name to draw the crowds. Of course, once again, this was the Lord's doing. Not only did it save us loads of money but it meant that we really did have to rely on local Christians and the delegates that we shipped in, inviting people along to the event, which at the end of the day proved to be a much better model.

The budget for Festival:Manchester was £1.5 million. This was on top of our ongoing and ever expanding Message budget, which had swelled to something similar. This meant that at a time when many other charities were feeling the pinch, we had to believe that our income in the year 2002–03 would more than double. Going into the year it felt daunting, and as the big week approached it was extremely scary. Yet by some miracle the bills have now all been paid.

Once again thousands of young people turned up from all over the world to serve and work on 315 community projects for Festival:Manchester. They did us proud and no job was too hard for them. This time there were many more projects run alongside the police (130 of them in all), who will now monitor their progress over the next 12 months. They will be looking for hardcore evidence that crime really does go down when this radical model of prayer and practical witness gets put into action. The first signs are already really encouraging and we are now working with the police to see how we can encourage the church of Jesus to be involved with these tough communities week in, week out and not just for one big annual bash. Police officers often witness young people at their very worst, so nothing can describe the impact on hardened officers when they see fantastic young people who never complain and take to every job, no matter how messy, with gusto and enthusiasm. I know that other police forces around the UK are looking on with interest, so who knows where this will lead?

During Festival:Manchester we used the same model we'd had in place at Soul Survivor – The Message 2000. There was worship, teaching and ministry in the mornings while delegates then got out on the projects in the afternoon and came back in the evening for big evangelistic gigs. This time, however, the evenings were situated in three big 3,000-seater venues right in the heart of the inner city, closer to where most of the projects were happening.

We planned to do these gigs for four nights before the huge party at the weekend. The first night we got off to a flying start, with dozens of young people coming to faith right across the venues. At our late-night leaders' meeting in a pub just round the corner from Heaton Park there was plenty of rejoicing. The second night, however, was altogether different. There was a weird, disruptive atmosphere at each venue: fights started to break out and a couple of young people were taken to hospital, one of our delegate coaches got a brick through the window and one of the local troublemakers was walking round with a hypodermic needle trying to stab people. When I preached in Salford it felt awful: I just couldn't seem to get the crowd's attention. They were shouting and fighting, and I came off stage feeling completely deflated. There was also hardly any response to the appeal. I know it's not all about numbers, but no response really is the pits for an evangelist.

When I eventually got to the leaders' meeting that night I found it was just the same in the other two venues. It was as if we'd gone right into the face of the enemy and really stirred something up. Some of the guys were literally in tears over the desperation of the young people we'd been trying to reach. I said that there was no way we were going to lose this battle. I told them that I'd call on the intercessors and that we'd be back in the pub the next night rejoicing again.

On the way home I phoned Debra Green, who was co-ordinating all the prayer for the mission. I told her the score and asked her to shift the whole thing up as many gears as it could go. The next day she did just that, emailing, phoning and texting intercessors all over the world to pray for us. She also arranged for several people (whom I would call proper, hardcore intercessors) to pray at each of the venues that evening. One Ugandan guy said later that he had not bound and loosed things like that since he was in Africa!

Just before I was about to preach, this time in the north zone in Moston, a local policeman came to me with a worried look on his face and told me that among the punters in the building that night were the Moston mafia. Great, I thought. Now we have some serious nutters in, who more than likely have guns and are intent on wrecking the whole thing.

However, I went on stage and preached, and there was an amazing sense of God's presence. Whole families, as well as loads of local young people, came to faith. Even more amazingly – as I found out later on that night – it was exactly the same in the other two venues. It really was as if we had broken through where it counts: in the heavenlies.

I had two thoughts on the back of all this hassle. First, I wondered how much of a threat to the enemy lots of our Christian gatherings are. Often I hear young people say that they went to such-and-such a Christian festival and it was like open heaven. Well, maybe it was. Maybe Satan backs off and is happy to let us have our 'bless ups' as long as they're altogether under the bowl. It's only as we get out and start to fight back in his territory, as we did at Festival:Manchester, that he starts to kick off. The other thing I wondered was how much emphasis we really put on prayer when we're organising our mission activities. I know in my heart that the real battle is won in prayer and that everything else is just the mopping-up operation. I agree with Oswald Smith when he says, 'Satan laughs at our work, mocks our toil, pours scorn on all our efforts but trembles when we pray.' But do I believe it enough to put my money where my mouth is? I'm totally convinced that if we're going to see the results we're after then we need to put more effort, more finance and more team into mobilising prayer and into pray-ers themselves than ever before.

While the delegates were grafting away on their projects across the city, a remarkable transformation was taking place at Heaton Park. A team of around 60 volunteer joiners were building the biggest skate park Manchester had ever seen. At the other end of the hill, Wigwam Acoustics, our events management team, were building a vast stage and video set-up to blast the message to the masses for the final gigs. Mike Spratt, the MD of Wigwam, who is also a good friend and long-time supporter of the Message, told me that even though they'd been doing this for about 20 years in the UK and had put up rigs for the likes of the Spice Girls, Blue, Westlife and Boyzone, they'd never done anything this big. I felt a sudden rush of pride. Not, I hope, because I'd helped put it on, but because the church of Jesus in Manchester was at last giving Him what He deserves: the very best.

As the weekend approached, one concern was the weather. I knew that if it rained at the weekend it would make a dramatic difference to crowd numbers. Every time I looked at Yahoo weather and saw a big black cloud and rain over Manchester for Saturday and Sunday I felt absolutely gutted. In my experience praying for the weather is a bit of a minefield. I've prayed my socks off for good weather for events we've organised in the past and they've been a wash-out. The slight problem, of course, is that you don't know whether a brother or sister is praying just as hard for the opposite weather to fit in with their plans.

Anyway, when faced with the black cloud scenario we got on with praying. Now, please don't blame me if it doesn't seem to work at your event, but the weather over the weekend was quite remarkable. Not only was it dry for the whole time, but there was a moment on the Saturday when the dreaded black clouds came over, but the wall of torrential rain stopped about 50 yards from where the crowds were gathered. I was with Luis in his caravan and he said that in 40 years of ministry he'd never seen anything quite like it. Shortly afterwards a beautiful rainbow arched above the arena and I was pleased that we'd called upon those African brothers to pray!

At the skate park there were incredible demos from a whole load of world class pros. After that Paul Johnson, who runs a ministry for skaters in the States, preached and then invited anyone who wanted to give their life to Christ to come onto the ramps to pray. Both days it was incredibly moving to see loads of skaters coming down the hill to become Christians. We also had a huge kids' zone, a car show, a food court and lots of sideshows to keep people entertained. The police told us that around 55,000 people attended over the weekend and, on top of the hundreds who came to know Jesus during the week, well over 1,000 responded to the good news in the park. What was fascinating was that around 50 per cent of those who responded had no church contact or Christian friends. I don't think that has ever happened before at a UK mission.

A real master stroke at Festival, on top of the big public response area, was to include a response tent, where we provided people with the opportunity to go for prayer throughout the day. Not only did many people come to know Jesus, but numerous sad, sick and suffering people were prayed for. It was exciting for us to see the wide range of people passing through the tent. It was obvious that we were cutting it with all sorts of ordinary, broken people in a way the church hasn't for generations, and these people included quite a few Muslims, Hindus and Jews who came to faith. Adrian Glasspole, who was part of our prayer and multi-cultural teams, works for Christian Mission to the Jews. The day after Festival he emailed me to say that he and his wife prayed they would be able to pray with five Jewish people. Sure enough, over the weekend they had the privilege of praying with the full five who came into the response tent. He finished his email by saying, 'Our God is an AWESOME God!' And he's dead right, of course.

Adrian's email was one of literally hundreds that hit our offices in the days following Festival, telling stories of salvation, healing and churches bursting at the seams with new believers. In hindsight it really does seem to be the most significant thing we've ever done, and it's now thrilling to realise that other cities and towns throughout the UK are looking to use this model in their own attempts to see their areas transformed.

Another legacy from Festival is renewed church unity. We had prayed for 500 partner churches from across the streams and denominations, and on the final Friday afternoon there was much whooping and hollering in the Festival office when the 500th partner church signed up. It seems to me that through all this mission activity many of these churches have had their eyes lifted and their faith expanded, so that now there's an excitement about a city being reached for Jesus, and that includes every aspect of the city – the business, the health scene, the politics, the leisure activities – all being transformed by the good news. That's the kind of faith that moves mountains in a city. We're not just looking for our little fellowship to grow. Yes, we are really taking ownership of our local area, but we are also lifting our sights to believe for the bigger picture of a whole area impacted for Jesus or, in the precious words of David in Psalm 37, we are believing for a land inherited and great peace enjoyed.

One more thing a few of us did in the build-up to Festival was get away for a couple of days with two big questions on the agenda. First, we wanted to know if it was time to expand our age range. For the first time at Festival we had gone beyond teenagers in our outreach work. Secondly, we were wondering if it was time to expand our geography. We'd made some great friends with leaders in other cities and several wanted us to help them work on stuff like Eden schools work, Planet Life and Festivals.

As we prayed together we strongly felt that after Festival it was right to bed back into working with young people. There were still plenty of them running riot in Manchester and it was obvious by looking at the statistics that if the church could keep the teenagers it had, never mind winning any new ones, we would be on our way to winning the nation for Jesus. Any business faced with a similar situation – where one area was pulling the whole thing down – would take immediate action and put resources into trying to sort the haemorrhaging out. It seemed right for us to do this.

We also felt that it was right to start working strategically with other cities, and we are now working closely with leaders in Liverpool and Sheffield to see how we can bless one another.

All in all, if we can keep our eye on the ball and God continues to bless what we're doing, the future looks quite exciting to me!

12

The Power of Partnership

There doesn't seem to be any way of writing this without it sounding dodgy, but over the years, I've met some amazing women. I'm not alone in this either, as William Booth (yes, Mr Salvation Army) was famous for saying, 'Some of my best men are women!' I'm not entirely sure of the exact qualities that so impressed Mr Booth, but I am sure that through a handful of inspiring women I have learnt many valuable lessons. Over time I have come to see that Christians – both as individuals and as groups – tend to succeed or fail on one specific point: partnership. As groups we move between the two extremes of unity or destruction. As individuals we face a choice between living life for ourselves or chasing after God with all we've got. Partnership is the key to success; if we sort it out things will move on.

In 1997 we went to South Africa to help Tearfund make a training video called *Desire*. As part of the trip we visited a township called Pietermaritzburg, and there I met an Indian nun who was living in the middle of one of the most violent parts of the world. In the area thousands of people have died from tribal warfare, and it remains the most intimidating place I have ever visited. Yet this old, poor nun chose to live in a minute shack with no running water and the threat of violence all around. Kids in rags were running in and out of her house and she literally glowed with love for Jesus. At the back of her home was a small chapel where people could come in, and she would give them communion and pray for them. The prayer time we had in there was totally inspiring, and we were all in awe of this remarkable woman.

I asked her what her ministry was, looking for the secret technique she had used to gain the respect and love of the locals. 'Just to be' was her reply. It turned out that she had never leafleted the area or put on any gigs. She simply was there, hanging out and giving her time and energy to whoever was in need. She made it a better place to live by being a radiant Christian in a very dark place, and despite the fact that she was softly spoken and about four feet tall, she made this loud-mouthed Manchester evangelist feel very, very small.

I remember meeting another woman from a totally different culture, whose background couldn't be further removed from that of the Indian nun in Pietermaritzburg: Baroness Caroline Cox, a 65-year-old grandmother, who is the deputy speaker in the House of Lords, and a woman who could so easily opt for living the high life. Instead she chooses to spend large parts of her life flying in rickety planes into the most dangerous parts of the world. She exposes torture and persecution, and brings to the world's attention the plight of Christians in countries such as Sudan, Burma, Afghanistan and North Vietnam. Again, she is a wonderful woman who has a dramatic effect on the world around her by choosing to go against the flow.

They are the kind of people who have understood just what it means to be a Christian. They are excited about being in partnership with God, and are prepared to make the sacrifice that is part of the deal. While your calling may not be to live in a township in South Africa or to fly off around the world and risk your life exposing persecution, God wants you all the same. He wants us to discover for ourselves how great (and tough) it is to be in partnership with Him. God has no hands but our hands, no feet but our feet and no mouth but our mouths. Without us on board Christianity struggles for workers.

I think my favourite verses at the moment are from Ephesians 3:20–21 where Paul says: 'Now to him who is able to do immeasurably more than all we ask or imagine, according to his power that is at work within us, to him be glory in the church and in Christ Jesus throughout all generations, for ever and ever!' These verses are about partnership, about God (who is able to do immeasurably more than all we can ask or imagine) being at work in us. I know that I can ask some pretty amazing things of God, and I can imagine some even more wildly exciting things that I might be too embarrassed to share with people, but God can do far more than anything I might be able to come up with. And how does He do these things? The good news is that it is not just by His power, but by His power in us, His partnership with us. To be in partnership with the living God is a seriously huge privilege, especially as it means getting used to doing big, eternal things. I believe that God wants people to get excited by the potential to be used by Him and start to make a difference. So what if the difference that you're going to make doesn't turn out to be the most public or noteworthy? We are all called to make a difference, to do our bit. From His perspective, God sees how all our efforts fit together, and He knows just how many anonymous works it takes to change a nation. The evangelist J. John pointed out that one snowflake can so easily melt on your cheek, but enough snowflakes together can stop traffic. That gives me hope that we can change the course of Britain, as long as we all get involved.

Apparently Mother Teresa was once approached by a cynical journalist who asked whether she really thought that her work could have an effect on poverty worldwide. Mother Teresa wisely replied that what she was doing may well be just a drop in the ocean, but that the ocean is made up of many drops. If we don't find our own place in God's incredible tapestry, we will not only miss out on a whole load of personal experiences and blessings, but we will do nothing to help prevent the rot that threatens to drag down even more lives than it has already. That God chooses to use dummies like us is a sure sign that He values these partnerships and longs to work through them even more. I believe that we are going to see increasing numbers of young people doing their bit and working together with God and each other. They are a generation who are growing up sick and tired of the disunity and lack of passion in the church, and with their radical commitment, the rewards could be massive.

A book landed on my doorstep a couple of weeks ago which detailed reports from around the world of amazing revivals that have been happening. I read through the chapters and was shocked to see a chapter about Manchester and our work. Deep in my heart I know that what's going on through us and around the city is a long way off from being considered full-blown revival. Yes, good things are happening – churches are coming to life and young people are coming to faith – but revival? We are seeing things that we haven't seen for a long time in the church in Manchester, and all the signs are there that if God sees fit, He could bring a massive move of His Spirit in this city; there is so much more to come. Thankfully the levels of excitement about the future are higher than I've ever experienced in my 25 years of being a Christian. There is a unity among the churches that for years and years was sadly lacking, but we must not let it go to our heads.

Eric Delve is an evangelist who has travelled all over the world preaching the gospel. He once said at an evangelists' conference that Manchester was the hardest place in which he had ever done mission. I have heard that Moody once had to cancel a mission in Manchester just because the churches were so disunited. While he was desperate for a little support to help him get out and preach, the local churches were busy arguing about who was going to introduce the evangelist and who was going to organise the committees. Churches are now starting to work together, so there is expectancy, there is unity and there is lots of prayer. Sir Fred Catherwood is President of the Evangelical Alliance, and on a recent visit to the city he described it as the most exciting meeting he had been to around the country, due largely to the sense of expectancy, the unity and the prayer.

The latest exciting thing that has been happening in Manchester is a new relevancy in the churches. Where once they were old, cold and half-full of Christians who wanted to get away from the world outside, now they are tailored to the people who need to hear the gospel the most. As they realise that church has to make sense to people on the street, so the petty religiosity seems to get left behind.

The Anglican church has been dosing up on some new life that has been going around it, but does that mean we should sit back and lamely wait for something exciting to come and knock on our door? What we should be doing instead is being a little more like the Reformers who shaped the church in the sixteenth century. Their motto was 'always reforming' as they pulled the church services out of Latin and into the language of the street. When Cranmer put his Church of England prayer book together, it was a radical street book in a language that people could understand. It communicated to a specific generation and brought the service up to date with the rest of contemporary culture. The problem is that most of the Reformers were burnt at the stake and, 350 years later, many of us are still using Cranmer's book.

Clearly the Salvation Army was once the most awesome organisation, used mightily by God. But the brass bands were the music of the streets 100 years ago. The tunes they played were the dance tunes of the day, and of course they received plenty of criticism and condemnation for it. It worked back then and managed to reach thousands of people, but today the tunes just don't seem to cut it. The Salvation Army, the Anglican church and even the movements that have only been around for 30 years or so all need to ask themselves if what they are doing is the best way of reaching the lost for Jesus. That's why I'm so thrilled that the Salvation Army have got a new bunch of radicals like Phil Wall coming through. They've picked up on the Eden project, and I wonder if there's a chance that, as Eden projects take off in Manchester, Edens everywhere could become a part of their work. Perhaps this could be a small part in turning the Salvation Army around from being the fastest declining movement to one that once again is seen as relevant in the tough places in the inner city.

The two posh southern churches I mentioned – Holy

Trinity, Brompton and Soul Survivor – are helping to perk things up in the Anglican church, and thankfully there are plenty of other churches and ministries queuing up to be a part of the action in other denominations. With increased expectancy, unity, prayer and relevancy, we are starting to get a firm foundation for God to move in. In themselves they are no guarantee of revival. Frustratingly, we must leave that to God.

13

The Meaning of Life

A friend of mine recently got back from a trip to Nigeria, where he had made some amazing discoveries. We're not talking about wildlife or woodcarvings here, but concrete evidence that God is on the move big time in Nigeria. He was invited there to speak at a night of prayer. Not too amazing, you may think, but when he turned up it soon became clear that this was no low-key affair. The prayer night was attended by a colossal one million people, all of whom were there to cry out to God from dusk till dawn. At around 11 o'clock at night a bell was rung and all the children were put to sleep under the benches, and on they went with their crying out to God. For most of the people, however, this was small-scale, as several weeks before there had been a prayer meeting that was reliably reported to have pulled in up to seven million people.

Understandably my mate was blown away by all this.

He was also curious, and went about tracking down the two men who were right at the heart of the revival. When he finally got to chat with them, he was desperate to find out exactly what they thought it was that had got (and kept) things going. He expected the answer to be something like prayer, unity or renewed holiness. But while each of those things was evident, he was surprised to get a different answer from the men. Independently of each other, both men told him that the reason behind this powerful move of God was just one thing: testimony.

Hearing this reminded me of that bit in Revelation 12 when Satan is thrown out and a loud voice in heaven says, 'They have overcome by the blood of the lamb and the word of their testimony.' Testimony is obviously a powerful thing, and the way that it has brought about a change in Nigeria is through people simply telling others about the good things they have seen God do. This in turn encourages people to expect God to do something great in their lives too, and before long there has been so much gossip about the gospel that people are longing to see exactly what God is going to get up to next.

I imagine that these testimonies started with people claiming that God had healed them from a headache or provided some little thing for them. Slowly, more dramatic stories would be told, as greater miracles were experienced, having an even greater impact on the audience. Once they got into the league of talking about how God had raised someone from the dead, then you can imagine how keen other people would be to meet up with God for themselves.

Once my mate had told me about his trip, we made sure that the next Planet Life service had plenty of room for testimony. We invited anyone to get up and tell the rest of us what good things God had done for them. The stories ranged from one girl who was on her deathbed when people prayed and she was healed to friends who had fallen out and had been reunited as they came to God and became Christians. There was a buzz as people shared the good things that God had done. I'll also never forget the first Planet Life after Festival:Manchester when, once again, we invited testimonies of what God had done during the festival. We had a stream of young people who had come to faith and were now going on in local churches. There was one little guy of about eight years old who had a major stutter and just about managed to say, 'I was m-m-m-miserable until I m-m-m-met J-J-J-Jesus.' As you can imagine the whole place erupted.

In a way this book is just my attempt at a testimony. I'm well aware that there are far better bands than the Tribe, far bigger ministries than the Message, far more spectacular miracles and faster growth happening, even in Britain, than we are seeing in Manchester, but God has done something and He deserves the glory. The thought of Edens spreading right across the tough parts of Manchester and on to other towns and cities across the UK is one that gets me and a whole load of other people excited.

Remember all that stuff about how important partnership is to us, how we need to hook up with God and be united with each other? The Eden projects have taken a new twist of late, and are now aiming to provide a service that gets right to the heart of many of the area's problems. Alongside the team of Christians who move in and work with young people in schools, on the streets and in the church, there will be central buildings that offer practical support. These LifeCentres will provide anything from professional counselling to drug rehabilitation, from pregnancy counselling to work on personal finances. Each Eden project will now follow this pattern, and we hope it will mean that we won't be just beating people over the head with a Bible, but actually meeting real needs, getting alongside people and showing them the love of Jesus through what we say and do.

There's a bloke I know called Terrence Rosalyn-Smith, who used to be a particularly wealthy international banker. He's still got cash, but now he uses it to set up projects in the inner city. When we first met, he told me how he was convinced that what young people need – especially the sort of damaged, dysfunctional young people we meet through the Eden projects – is to find out exactly what they are worth. He went on to explain that he felt there were three key areas in which this needed to happen. First, they need to be aware of the fact that they have a solid community around them; secondly, they need to find their value in work; and thirdly, through worship, they need to realise that there is a God who made them and loved them enough to die for them. Terrence went on to explain that he knew his part in the plan was to set up small businesses in the inner city that would take on the often unemployable young people who live there. It struck him that what we were trying to do with Eden was to accomplish the other two goals – the worship and the community – so why not join up and go for all three? Something about what he said made perfect sense, and we realised that the idea had phenomenal potential. By moving the Christians in and getting them to spend time with the locals we were catering for the spiritual well-being of the young people, and by helping them get back to work as well as dealing practically with other problems they face we should have a much greater chance of seeing long-term change.

At the heart of our idea to have 300 workers getting stuck into Eden projects is a belief that we need people who will make a big statement to others by living in a way which is opposite to the spirit of the age. We want to see people who are turning their back on this incredibly materialistic world in which we live, moving out of their nice pads and into a grotty place simply because they love Jesus. It's a movement that God is all over and one that I'm glad He has promised to bless.

Shopping is now the number one leisure activity in the UK and the shopping centres have become the new places of worship. In past generations, close proximity to a church was a key thing in most people's choice of where to live. These days the important thing seems to be being near Tesco's, Sainsbury's or Dixon's. How sad is that?

The main problem is that today's society lives in the shadow of an enormous false god; a god that even Christians bow down and submit their lives to. The god's name is money, and not surprisingly worshipping it always results in bitter disappointment. We live in the most materialistic age in history, and David Watson, who I believe was an awesome man of God, had something like this to say about it:

> There has been a great attack on the Eastern church in the twentieth century. That attack is persecution, and it has failed miserably. You can't persecute the church out of existence. You just crush it and it comes back stronger than ever before. And yet the great attack on the Western church in the twentieth century has been materialism. Materialism has been such a success for the enemy.

David Watson was right, and sadly the church has suffered for the attacks. Materialism has managed to squeeze the life out of plenty of Christians, many of whom have honestly believed that happiness is linked to possessions. At the heart of Eden is the desire to live in the opposite spirit of an age which says 'more more more for me'. Instead of all this greed, we're keen to take on the idea of more for Jesus and more for the poor who burn so intensely on His heart.

I'm finishing writing this little book in the run-up to Christmas. I don't want to appear a misery guts, but once again I'm struck by how pathetic much of the hype around this season is, as people desperately flog around trying to buy things for people who actually have more than enough of everything. Meanwhile, around the world hundreds of millions of people starve and every moment dozens of people die of diarrhoea and other easily preventable diseases. What a messed-up world we live in, where greed is so readily accepted.

Of course, few would admit to such a vice. I mean, it seems like such an obvious trap, doesn't it? The truth is that loads of us have signed up for 'things' instead of signing up for God. It's not limited to rich people either. I know plenty of poor people who are locked into a cycle of believing that if they get the things, happiness won't be far behind. You need only watch the queues in the Wythenshawe newsagents' on a Saturday night at 6.45 p.m. to see loads of desperate people buying a fistful of lottery tickets with their last fiver in an attempt to get happy. They're there each week, despite the ultra-slim chances of them winning more than they've spent, as well as all the evidence that actually winning the prize jackpot often leads to unhappiness and paranoia.

As George Michael summed up the dilemma in one of his early solo songs, 'What does a young boy do when all his dreams come true?' He certainly had all he ever wanted – money, sex and power – but not only was it not enough, it was actually an unpleasant situation to be in. It really is a terrible place to be when all your dreams have come true and you find it's still not enough. That's why so many millionaires and superstars we fawn over turn to increasingly wacky lifestyles, desperately trying to fill that hole in their lives that can only be filled by Jesus.

If this book makes you think about one thing, I hope it is this: getting sucked into the race for more possessions is a waste of time. Life is not made up of acquisitions, but of inspirations – spending more time with God will make you happier than spending more cash. Of course God doesn't mind us having some things – He doesn't mind us owning nice things – but I'm sure you have heard it said before that those things can so quickly own us. Unless we 'seek first the kingdom of God' we are not going to get all the other things that God has got stored up for us. Those things might not be possessions, but they will be all the things we really need to live a fulfilled and contented life.

So what exactly is a young boy or girl to do? I'm sure that one of the best ways of combating the powerful grip of money is to give it away. This isn't just about giving away 10 per cent (although I'm staggered at how many young Christians can't even countenance the idea of giving away 10 per cent of their income) and keeping the rest, but giving as a response to the incredibly extravagant love that God has poured out on us. There are many young people around who are kidding themselves by saying that when they get older they'll give money away. The trouble is that when that big wad does land up in your wallet, it's pretty hard to break the habit of keeping hold of it. I admit that it can seem foolish to be giving money away when you're struggling yourself, but there's always someone worse off than yourself, and we can always give till it hurts. Besides, whoever said that Christianity was supposed to be easy?

There are many Christian business people who start out with the best possible intentions, planning one day to give stacks of cash to God's work. But the day never seems to come along and, sadly, God's gift of the skills of the entrepreneur isn't used to its full potential. I'm not anti entrepreneurs; in the ideal world those gifts would allow them to enjoy some of their money and give even more of it away to help support God's work. But many of these Christian business people fall into the trap of living just beyond their means. Instead of settling for one particular house, car or holiday destination they feel the need to constantly upgrade to a better model. With all these financial pressures bearing down upon the wallet, there can be no wonder that the idea of giving a large proportion of it away seems to make so little sense.

I am convinced that God wants to raise up a new generation of business people: those who are focused on mission and reaching people with the gospel. These money-makers will be incredibly successful at raising funds, but the priority and focus of their lives won't be money for themselves or their next business venture, but cash for the kingdom.

Jesus said these scary words in Matthew 6:19–24, and they're clear enough not to need any commentary. As I read them they always remind me of what I am really like.

Do not store up for yourselves treasures on earth, where moth and rust destroy, and where thieves break in and steal. But store up for yourselves treasures in heaven, where moth and rust do not destroy, and where thieves do not break in and steal. For where your treasure is, there your heart will be also. The eye is the lamp of the body. If your eyes are good, your whole body will be full of light. But if your eyes are bad, your whole body will be full of darkness. If then the light within you is darkness, how great is that darkness! No-one can be a slave to two masters. Either you will hate the one and love the other, or you will be devoted to the one and despise the other. You cannot be a slave to both God and Money.

Now it could be that what you've been reading over the previous few pages has upset you a little (if it has, that probably means you're normal). There are others in the church who would probably be even more upset about it, though, especially as they consider personal wealth to be a sign of God's blessing. This 'prosperity gospel' suggests that if you give some of your wedge to the church or a particular ministry, you will receive a hundred times that amount as a return blessing from God. While in some ways this is quite true – we do know that God loves to bless us – it kind of ignores the fact that those blessings come prepacked with a whole load of persecutions and difficulties. What's more, Jesus told us to store up our treasures in heaven rather than on the earth, and I don't think that it takes a genius to work out that BMWs probably won't be on God's list of

eternal blessings in heaven. It only takes a little time to read through the Gospels to discover that instead of being full of followers who were dripping with gold, Jesus' disciples were poor and, later, persecuted.

Few would doubt that Paul was the greatest Christian that ever lived. Towards the end of his life he was able to say (in Philippians 4) that he had known what it was to be in plenty, yet he had also known what it was to be in want. The prosperity gospel seems to sign up for the first half and neatly ignore the second. What is more, Paul isn't only talking about cash, but about safety. Among the times when he was 'in want' were the three times when he was beaten with rods and the five times in which he received 39 lashes. He was shipwrecked on three separate occasions and was in constant danger whenever he was on the move. He had struggled and toiled, he often went without sleep, and had known hunger, cold and nakedness. Paul's testimony is hardly in line with a triumphalistic prosperity gospel view; hardly a great example of the three Cs (Christ, Cash and Comfort). Paul had known both sides of the coin, bu the things that were most precious to him were god ness and contentment. Paul encouraged others to cha after the same goal, believing that in pursuing go ness, contentment would not be far behind. Paul did couple godliness with wealth or success, but with most elusive and indefinable of blessings: happiness

If you read Revelation 12 you come across a bit v the devil is cast down and the people of God are v ous in the name of Jesus. The passage explains tha

victory over the devil comes through the blood of the Lamb and by their testimony. It also points out that these believers did not love their own lives even in the face of death. In other words, they knew their place.

That's the great need of the hour: a group of people who have got hold of the cross, who know what sacrifice is all about. For these people the realisation that God loved them enough to die for them will carry them through all manner of difficulties. We need these people to not be shy about proclaiming their faith and testifying about the good things God has done. They need to be the sort of people whose hearts and minds are not set on possessions but on living for eternity. Like Paul, they are sure to come up against beatings, dangers and poverty, but hopefully they will be able to repeat his words from 2 Corinthians 4: 'We fix our eyes not on what is seen, but on what is unseen. For what is seen is temporary, but what is unseen is eternal.'

I was involved in my first mission a few weeks after I became a Christian. It was in Manchester in 1978, and David Watson was heading it up. Before we went out on the streets one night, a guy called Will Rogers came along to give us a pep talk. I'll never forget what he said: 'When I die, I want to hear the trumpets blowing from the angels and I want to see the saints dancing. I want to hear them say, "Come in, Will. Enter the joy of the Lord." I want a massive party because I have done stuff for Jesus. Despite all my imperfections I want to have made a splash.'

A few weeks after he said those words to us I walked

into the Scripture Union shop and saw a little picture of Will Rogers. Underneath was a handwritten message that he had died a few days before, and above it were the words 'Good and faithful servant'. I could almost hear the champagne corks popping in heaven.

That's it – that's what life is all about. Satan doesn't want us to realise it, but this life is just a breath, a mere few seconds and a speck in all eternity. The only things that will last are those that will be remembered in heaven. Forget the cash or the labels; it's only what's done for Jesus that matters. So let's live like it.

In 1990 my dad died after a struggle with heart disease that lasted several years. As he lay in bed during his final hours, fighting for breath, he asked my mum to sing to him. She chose that slightly cheesy old chorus 'Turn your eyes upon Jesus'. One part of it reads, 'look full in His wonderful face, and the things of earth will grow strangely dim in the light of His glory and grace,' and as she sang, the presence of God came into the room and my dad calmed down. They spent the rest of the night singing their way through the *Mission Praise* songbook, and in the early hours of the morning my dad sang his way out of this world and into the next.

When he died, my mum saw a picture in her mind of Jesus coming into their bedroom and picking my dad up. He carried him into a beautiful garden where she heard some familiar voices. Some she recognised as belonging to his Christian friends, but one stuck out as the voice of his brother, who had died the year before. As she listened, my mum heard them saying to my dad,

'Hey, George, come in. Look at this! It's wonderful here!'

At the end of the day that's what really counts. When put in that context, wacky things like Eden make loads of sense.

14

Postscript: End Thoughts

Before I finally get round to signing off this book, there are a couple more things I need to say. I have been praying that there will be people who read it who will want to respond to stuff that God's been saying to them. Among you, there might be some potential Eden workers who will move long term into the inner city of Manchester. As you have read this book, and maybe as you have heard about Eden in other places, you've thought that this is what you want to do with your life. You're at a point in your life where you can make a big decision; one that will mean turning your back on the materialistic culture we live in and living alongside the poor and the broken for Jesus. If that is you – if you believe that God is maybe calling you to be one of the 300 people who will move into the inner city of Manchester over the next few years – please write to our office: The Message, PO BOX 151, Manchester M22 4YY, or email us at info@message.org.uk

We'll send you all the information about Eden, an application pack with details about the churches we're working with, the areas we are working in, and the whole vision of Eden. We take up loads of references and spend a long time moving people through the selection process, so don't expect to be packing your bags just yet. It's a tough calling, and the vast majority of people who apply don't end up moving in, but if you believe that you could be one of the few, get in touch. You might, however, feel that you're not quite ready for Eden yet, but you want to get in on the action in Manchester. Xcelerate, our five-month evangelist training school, could be just what you're looking for. If so, we'd also love to hear from you. Just contact the office and we'll send you all the stuff.

The other group of people I want to address at the very end of this book are those who still aren't Christians. Why miss out any longer? If you have read this book and you've spoken to other Christians, maybe you've heard the Christian message before but still haven't responded. Responding right now would be a very good thing to do. If you're not ready for that, why not pray and ask God, if He's really there, to help you get to know Him? When you've said that, read a Gospel from the Bible (I suggest either Mark or John in the New Testament). Read it with an open mind. As you read it, I believe that God will speak to you and you will realise that Jesus was no ordinary man, but that He really was God come down to earth on an incredible rescue mission. You will find as you read it that you will get confronted by Jesus, a guy who spoke the most amazing words. In fact, those words were so amazing that in 2,000 years no one has been able to improve them. The words He spoke then are still firing people up today. Read the Gospels and you will find out that He proved it by doing the most amazing miracles. Jesus really did put His hands on blind eyes so they could see and on deaf ears so they could hear. He brought dead people back to life on a number of occasions, and even His enemies couldn't deny His extraordinary powers.

Most importantly, you will find that you are confronted by someone who loved you enough to die for you. The weird thing about Jesus is that the most important event in His life was His death. It was more important than all the times He spoke to huge crowds, and more important than all the times He healed people. It sounds strange, but when He was on the cross He was taking the full force of God's anger for all the wrong stuff in your life. Jesus was punished for all your rotten thoughts, attitudes and actions. The Bible calls Him our substitute; in other words, He came in our place. I know that I deserve to be punished for all the wrong things I've done, but Jesus was punished in my place and that is fantastically good news. When you get hold of it, it's enough to keep you going for all eternity.

There are no special words or ceremonies to go through to become a Christian. It's simply a matter of turning away from anything that is wrong in your life, believing that Jesus is the Son of God and that on the cross He took the punishment for all that is wrong in your life, and asking Him to take control of your life. He will not force His way in. But if you want to give Him everything, if you are prepared to commit your life to Jesus today, He will come in. I know that loads of people in Manchester and all over the world find it helpful to say a little prayer in order to say 'yes' to God, to tell Him that they're really serious about it all. This is a prayer I suggest you use if you want to do just that:

> Lord Jesus, I want to follow You. I know I've done loads of bad things. I know that I don't deserve to go to heaven. I'm sorry and I turn away from everything that I know is wrong in my life. Thank You so much for dying on the cross for me. Thank You for taking the punishment for all the wrong things I've done. Please take away all the rubbish in my life and fill me with Your Holy Spirit. With Your help, Lord Jesus, I'll live all out for You for the rest of my life. Amen.

It is because Jesus really is alive that, as you pray that prayer and mean it, He will come into your life.

After Jesus died, His body was put in a tomb and a massive stone was rolled across the entrance. Once again He proved that He was who He said He was, and that He had beaten death once and for all, because He came back to life and walked around for nearly six weeks. He was seen by hundreds of people and then went back to heaven and sent His Holy Spirit to live inside every real Christian to help us live the best life possible, and to let us know we will go to heaven when we die. The Christian life is one that is full of sacrifice, commitment and hard work. It's also a life of contentment and power. This power is available both when we're alive and when we're dead as, like Jesus, we too will go to heaven one day. Jesus said this: 'You will know me and you will know eternal life.' He meant that if we hook up with Him, He throws eternal life into the deal.

If you did pray that prayer, please write in to the Message office at PO Box 151, Manchester M22 4YY as we would love to send you some literature to help you go on with God.

Resources Available from the Message

Fresh (video, DVD, book)

The latest discipleship resource from the Tribe, looking closely at what God has to say about some of the big issues in life. The video has six chunky sessions, plus full-length pop features. The book is the essential accompaniment to get young people going deeper with God.

Fresh (video)	£12.99
Fresh (book)	£ 4.99
Fresh (video and 6 books)	£29.99
Fresh (DVD)	£15.99
Fresh (DVD and 6 books)	£32.99

Raise Your Game (album)

The awesome album from the Tribe, featuring 15 brand-new tracks and over an hour of God-centred music to lift your spirits and move your feet.

Raise Your Game (album)   £9.99

Nobody's Child – **John Robinson**

John Robinson had the worst possible start in life. Taken into care at four months old, he was left in abusive foster homes for most of his childhood. At 14 he was sent to a detention centre for arson. Heading towards a life of crime, he moved from borstal to the streets to psychiatric hospital, a scared, tattooed, broken and angry young man. Yet today John heads up the Message's Eden Bus ministry and does a remarkable work for God in inner-city Manchester. Here is the amazing story of that transformation.

Nobody's Child   £6.99

Festival: Manchester **(DVD)**

This DVD gets you close up to all the action from 'on the streets' and 'in the park'. It's jam-packed with nearly an hour of footage from this awesome event. As well as the stories from the streets, there's music from Toby Mac, LCGC, the Tribe, thebandwithnoname, Tim Hughes, Matt Redman and more. This is your chance to bring a little piece of Festival:Manchester into your living room.

Festival: Manchester (DVD)   £12.99

Xcelerate – *The Evangelist's Heartbeat* by Matt Wilson and Andy Hawthorne

Xcelerate, the evangelist training school, has its home in Manchester and provides fired-up young disciples with the opportunity to learn about reaching this generation. This book contains valuable lessons from well-known evangelists, plus down-to-earth stories straight from the streets, featuring wise words and strange tales from Andy Hawthorne, J. John, Mike Pilavachi, Roy Crowne, Mark Ritchie, Ness Wilson, Colette Smethurst, Paul Gutteridge, Matt Wilson and the girls and guys of Xcelerate.

Xcelerate (book)   £6.99

We're constantly updating and introducing new products to help you get closer to God. For the full range check out www.message.org.uk

We'd love to put you on our mailing list to keep you bang up-to-date with everything that's going on. Just contact the office on info@message.org.uk or call 0161 946 2300.

The Message Trust
PO Box 151
Manchester
M22 4YY
Tel: 0161 946 2300   Email: info@message.org.uk

Red Moon Rising by **Pete Greig** – 24-7 is at the centre of a prayer revival across the globe and this book gives a fantastic insight into what God is doing with ordinary prayer warriors.

Passion for Your Name by **Tim Hughes** – To read this book is to share in a journey of discovery, of truths encountered, principles gleaned, mistakes made and lessons learned. A valuable companion for all worshippers!

The Truth Shall Set You Free by **Beth Redman** – This book is unashamedly about God, His heart for us, His love and mercy shown to us, and His promises made to us. It's the truth of knowing God that will heal us and ultimately bring contentment and peace to our lives.

Wasteland? by **Mike Pilavachi** – Mike Pilavachi draws on his own experience and the Bible to infuse faith, hope and love in us, and inspire us on our journey.

The Heart of Worship Files by **Matt Redman** – This book features highlights from the very popular website, heartofworship.com. Compiled by Matt Redman, it will encourage and inspire you to help others reach new depths of worship.

survivor